The Story of Ewha

From History to Future

The Story of Ewha

From History to Future

Ewha Archives

Ewha Womans University Press

Foreword

This book revisits the history of the time-honored institution of Ewha, which since its founding in 1886 as Korea's first school for women has continued to develop into one of the nation's largest, most prestigious universities. *The Story of Ewha: From History to Future* is part of an effort to commemorate Ewha's founding spirit and history, and to share its vision for the future.

Since Mary F. Scranton founded Ewha, the school has been carrying out its calling as a place of learning for the women of Korea. Under its grand vision of "the humanization of women," Ewha has accompanied women pioneers in their myriad challenges and accomplishments as the firsts in their fields.

Now Ewha is opening a new page in its history as the global hub for women's education, producing talented international women possessing intellect and character.

The history that Ewha has created over the past 127 years is the mirror that sheds light on its exciting and brilliant future, for Ewha's history has always been based on its spirit of service and devotion, of sharing and caring, and of challenge and new frontiers.

Ewha's history has been made by pioneers unafraid of new challenges. They have courageously stepped out into unexplored territories, armed with an awareness of their calling as required by the society and the times. Many of Ewha's accomplishments were "firsts," achieved only by standing up against social prejudices against women. Those of us at Ewha can proudly declare that throughout the turmoil of Korea's modern history, Ewha has built a strong foundation for the humanization of women. Ewha has pushed women to the forefront as agents of history, and through its future-minded educational vision, has produced numerous women experts who have pioneered new frontiers in their respective fields.

What enabled such challenges and achievements was Ewha's spirit of service and sharing. The teachers and alumnae of Ewha, geared with a sense of Christian calling, have been moving forward with their vision to pull Korean women out of patriarchal oppression, to the forefront of society and history. Ewha began with one small opportunity of learning offered to a girl living in alienation. The spirit of serving and caring for the oppressed and the weak is the singular learning that Ewha always has, and will continue to, uphold.

Rooted in this historical legacy, Ewha's spirit of service and sharing has opened a new page in its history as the global hub for women's education. Ewha's new vision for the calling of these new times comprises providing education and service for women of the Third World suffering from poverty and oppressions of the patriarchal order, and building a global communal Ewha network that reaches all parts of the world.

Ewha's history has up to now been complied in a series of publications including *70 Years of Ewha's History*; *80 Years of Ewha's History*; *100 Years of Ewha's History*; and *Ewha Old and New: 110 Years of History 1886–1996*. While these books served as expansive and detailed accounts of historical facts, *The Story of Ewha* aims to offer to readers both inside and outside the Ewha community a more accessible resource to tap into Ewha's long history and its proud values.

History does not lie merely within the past. History is the seed of our identity, the soil of our future vision. The Ewha spirit, which has led this institution through its great history, will live on in its future as Ewha, in the face of new changes and challenges, moves forward with its new vision as the global hub for women's education.

September 2013
Kim Sun-Uk
President
Ewha Womans University

1886 梨花 女大 1945

眞 美 善

EWHA W.U.

Table of Contents

Ⅲ. Ewha College 1925-1945 Half-Century of Miracles

Ⅳ. Ewha Womans University 1945-1961 Standing Tall in the Face of Hardship

Ⅴ. Progress and Growth 1961-1979 Establishment of Academic Tradition

1886

1910

I
Ewha Haktang Years

Break of a New Dawn

: Ewha Archives

Pear Blossom School

One spring day in May of 1886, a young woman wearing her hair in a bun, as was the custom for married women, arrived in a palanquin chaperoned by servants, at the gate of a traditional roof-tile house perched atop a hill in the Jeong-dong neighborhood in downtown Seoul, abloom with soft white pear blossoms. Introducing herself as a concubine of a high government official, the woman stated that she wanted to learn the English language and serve as an interpreter for the Queen of Joseon. As she listened, American missionary Mary F. Scranton found it hard to respond in words. But soon she opened her arms wide, her face flushed with emotion, and the two women embraced.

For Scranton, it was a long-awaited moment, coming after

many months spent in setting up her school and praying for the arrival of her first student. For many years her fellow missionaries had toiled hard on this barren land and now their efforts would finally bear fruit. This first student, whose name remains in records only as Lady Kim, would leave the school only after three months due to an illness, but on this day, her visit launched the beginning of women's education in Korea as Ewha Haktang accepted its inaugural student as the country's first school for women. The date May 31 is still commemorated today as the founding day of Ewha Womans University.

It was a year earlier, in June 1885, that Scranton first set foot on the Korean peninsula, where she had been sent by the Woman's Foreign Missionary Society of the Methodist Episcopal Church to initiate projects for the women of Asia. In this unfamiliar land, where even chicken and eggs "only looked like those at home but tasted very different," Scranton had been pursuing education and medical service. Her plans in Korea included founding a school for the girls of this country, deprived of education opportunity due to social conventions, and opening a professional clinic exclusively for women, who had been taught within the Confucian tradition to avoid male doctors. Achieving these goals would contribute to the development of women as members of the nation's workforce, which Scranton believed to be her calling and her mission, shared by early Prot-

Ewha Haktang Founder Mary F. Scranton.

Ewha Haktang's first school building, a traditional *hanok* built in 1886.

estant missionaries to Korea.

Mary Scranton's plans, however, faced many hardships from the start. Recruiting students proved especially difficult. Joseon dynasty did not allow women the same education opportunities as men and most Koreans were also extremely guarded against Westerners. The Confucian faith had resulted in a closed society where few parents would willingly entrust their daughters to a complete stranger, a foreigner at that. Girls from poor homes were just as difficult to approach as noblewomen tucked away in the deep corners of the women's quarters. There were even macabre rumors that Westerners sucked the blood of children and plucked out their eyes, or kidnapped them to be sold to a faraway country. Scranton had to plead to the parents of prospective students, offering care and accommodations for their daughters.

Ewha Haktang's first long-term pupil was a girl named Ggotnim, whose enrollment was secured by a signed agreement with her mother never be taken out of the country without parental consent. Esther Park, who later studied in the U.S. and became Korea's first woman physician, recalled the day she first arrived at the school under her maiden name Kim Jeom-dong, as follows:

I was ten years old when I went to meet Mrs. Scranton. It

> was a very cold day so she told me to sit close to the heating stove, and I was overcome with fear that she would push me into the stove and burn me to ashes. Her kind and beautiful face, however, made me cast away such thoughts.

There came an event, in February of 1887, that finally put an end to such rumors and misconceptions. King Gojong bestowed the school with the official name Ewha Haktang—meaning Pear Blossom School. This meant that Joseon's government had acknowledged the institution as a public school, expressing trust in the missionaries who ran it.

Unfortunately, no signboards carrying the name Ewha Haktang from the school's early years remain today, but this new title must have carried great authority, for it clearly helped quell the fearsome stories and rumors associated with the school.

There are several speculations about the origins of the name Ewha, but the most persuasive seems to be related to the pear orchard on the hills of Jeong-dong where the school first opened. Old maps show that there was an orchard on the site named Ewha-jeong, or Pear Blossom Garden, which presumably resulted in the proliferation of pear trees in the area.

This was a site that offered some of the most scenic views in all of Seoul and now it housed a special new school that would witness the blossoming of great knowledge and learning.

: The main gate at Ewha Haktang, with
the school's official signboard bestowed by King Gojong.

Ewha Haktang's Early Years

As its founder and inaugural principal, Mary F. Scranton had managed to recruit students despite the unsupportive environment surrounded by rumors, but it was no easy task taking care of the young children on her own. Ewha's first students spent their days learning the Lord's Prayer and hymns or playing games, without structured classes. There was no distinction between studying and playing, and the school functioned more as a foster care facility that provided food, clothing and accommodation. Ewha Haktang naturally took the form of a boarding school, one where all tuition and living expenses were free of charge.

It was after Louisa C. Rothweiler, an experienced missionary teacher, succeeded Scranton as principal that the school began to establish its curriculum and administration system. Academic subjects were formally categorized to raise the standard of the education offered and school regulations were reinforced. These changes allowed the students to be trained in the modern academic disciplines of geography, mathematics, science, English reading, and grammar.

As the student population grew and additional teachers were hired, strict distinctions were made between classes and dormitory routines, adding structure and discipline to school life. According to records from 1896, ten years after the school's opening, each school day began with breakfast at 7 a.m., followed by classes from 8 to noon, then lunch and prayer, and afternoon classes from 1 to 4 p.m. Young students took recess before dinner, for games like marbles and seesaw jumping, while the older students helped with work around the dormitory. After dinner, all students devoted 15 minutes to prayer in their rooms to wrap up the day.

Since the girls lived in dorms, off-campus excursions were highly anticipated events. Heading to Chungdong First Methodist Church for service each Sunday offered an opportunity to see the outside world, but the most exciting event was the school picnic, which was arranged once or twice a year. In the spring, the students enjoyed flowers blossoming on the grounds of the majestic mansion Seokpa-jeong, situated outside Jaha

Gate north of the city, or took the streetcar to Hongneung Royal Tombs outside the city's East Gate. Beautiful foliage provided the occasion for outings in the fall. On the days of Ewha student excursions, pedestrians stopped to watch the parade of girls wearing traditional *hanbok*, matched in crimson as school uniform.

Ewha Haktang continued to grow with increasing public support and acceptance. Student population, which began with four girls, increased to 12 in the following year, then to 28 four years later, and in 1895, exceeded the building's capacity and the school was no longer able to take in all the students that sought enrollment. Now there were students who were willing to pay tuition to attend school, which marked a turning point for the school as a genuine educational institution.

This development owed much to the commitment and devotion of the missionaries but was also driven by social change. At the time, the Independence Club had been established to preserve Korea's integrity amidst the clamor among colonial powers on the peninsula, its ideology based on egalitarianism and gender equality gaining consensus from the public.

An anecdote from 1896, of an enthusiastic married woman who paid a visit to Ewha Haktang speaks for this change. The woman, possessing a strong faith that women were important assets that contributed to national strength, desperately wanted

⁚ Students during Ewha Haktang's early years.

a chance to study at Ewha. The missionaries, however, rejected her request, citing the lack of classroom space and the school regulations that barred married women from admission. But the woman would not relent as she raised an extinguished lantern in her servant's hand, "There is darkness in my country, dark like this blown-out lantern. Mothers should receive learning to teach their children. What are we to do?" The school, impressed by the visitor's passionate spirit, decided to admit her, accepting her proposal to pay full tuition and expenses. This woman was Hah Ran-sa, who went on to become the first Korean woman to earn a bachelor's degree in the U.S., returning to teach at Ewha and winning wide recognition as an activist.

This inspired many other married women to seek education at Ewha, which resulted in the school's decision in 1908 to admit married women, in respect of their determination to receive a modern education and become a strong contributor to their family and society.

Medical Service for and by Women

In winter of 1887, women were frequently seen entering the Korean-style building on the grounds of Ewha Haktang, their faces discreetly covered with traditional head dress. They had come seeking treatment at the first clinic for women in Korea, which offered services by a woman doctor. Later given the official name Boguyeogwan, or the Center for the Care and Treatment of Women, the clinic was the fruit of Mary Scranton's vision to provide not only education but medical service to women in Korea.

There had been services offered by a female doctor or nurses at Jejungwon, Korea's first hospital practicing modern Western medicine, but social customs at the time called for a strict segregation between men and women, which made it hard for the women to freely seek medical help. The lack of specialized women's medicine also made treatment difficult.

For a while, Principal Scranton's son William B. Scranton, a physician, offered free service at his home as part of a public health project, putting up a sign outside his door that read, "Men, women, young or old, are invited to seek treatment from an American doctor, whatever affliction you might be suffering from. Please visit at 10 in the morning and bring an empty bottle."

But it was not easy for women to seek the assistance of a male American physician. Scranton and her son made a strong case to the headquarters of the missionary society that a female doctor was needed in Korea, which resulted in the dispatch of Meta Howard, a physician from Chicago. An exclusive and professional hospital for women was now ready to open in Korea thanks to the Methodist Episcopal Church's mission in the service of women.

Under Principal Scranton's supervision, Boguyeogwan began operation on the Jeong-dong campus. The two institutions complimented each other since Scranton's initiatives in education and in medicine were closely related, as seen in the examples of Byeoldan, Ewha's second student who enrolled in the school after visiting the clinic seeking treatment, and of Kim Lucy, who encountered students playing on the lawn when she

Boguyeogwan, Korea's first hospital exclusively serving women, opened in 1887.

The Nurse Training Center at Ewha Haktang was a pioneer in the education of women in the medical profession.

Esther Park, Korea's first woman physician.

accompanied her aunt on a medical appointment and begged her father to send her to school.

Ewha Haktang and Boguyeogwan functioned as sister institutions that worked together and supported each other. The clinic took care of the students' health, while the students contributed to the clinic by helping at the pharmacy or serving as interpreter. The medical staff at the clinic took on lectures at the school, introducing the students to the world of modern science. The clinic also opened roads to new professions for women, as nursing assistants, or as Bible women who read the scriptures to in-patients to spread the word.

The operation of Boguyeogwan led Scranton to found Korea's first nurse training center. Here is how a magazine portrayed this new school, which provided medical and nursing education for women when the term "nurse" had yet to exist in the Korean vocabulary:

> In Seoul's Daejeong-dong area, there is a hospital for women called Boguyeogwan, which provides devoted care for afflicted women, and the school also operates the Nurse Training Center... It offers excellent education to a selected group of intelligent women, carried out by outstanding doctors and teachers, teaching them the various types of illnesses and the different work involved in nursing, helping the students experience treatment methods through

> observing, listening and hands-on practice... Studying for this profession is of higher importance for women of Korea than of other countries, so we hope that young, meticulous women will enroll at this school and study hard through tests and practices instead of letting their youth dwindle away, thereby accomplishing many great things.
>
> \- *The Home Magazine*, Vol. 1 No. 4, Sept. 25, 1906

Two Ewha Haktang graduates became the first professionally trained Korean nurses at the center's inaugural capping ceremony in 1906, a milestone in the history of nursing in Korea.

Ewha Haktang and Boguyeogwan, in their early years, were indispensable to each institution's vision and agenda. Ewha was able to cultivate Korea's first women physicians and open a medical school immediately following Korea's liberation from Japanese colonial rule in 1945 because Boguyeogwan had laid the foundation for the school in the field of medicine. And it was thanks to the tradition and system established by the Nurse Training Center that Ewha launched Korea's first undergraduate department in nursing in 1955.

Outcry of Korean Women

The year 1908 marked a meaningful turning point in Ewha's history. On June 18, the school produced its first graduating class in 23 years. The five students were the first to complete the middle school curriculum established four years earlier. On commencement day, they all dressed in traditional *hanbok* that was white like pear blossoms, their hair worn up, and headed for the ceremony at the Chungdong First Methodist Church.

Their completion of the middle school program signified that an Ewha student's graduation no longer meant that she was getting married. Previously, a commencement ceremony had been unthinkable at the school. The first students at Ewha Haktang were of varying age groups when they started out, but when they reached 15 or 16, they were expected to leave school to get married. In some rare cases, of course, a student left to pursue higher education overseas, but most returned home for marriage.

When their daughters reached this age, the parents grew anxious, so in some cases the missionaries took matters into their own hands. The Ewha faculty would look for husbands for their students and make wedding preparations, even host formal traditional wedding ceremonies.

The students, however, having acquired a modern education at Ewha, faced conflicts and confusions. A diary entry by Esther Park vividly captures the torments and anxieties that these girls suffered, caught between their present lives and the future they envisioned:

> For three sleepless nights I agonized over this issue. I am not fond of men, nor am I good at sewing. Our customs, however, require marriage. I cannot do anything about this, in spite of the fact that I dislike men. If God intends to make this Park my husband, then I shall become his wife even if my mother disapproves of him. I've told my mother, "What difference does it make whether he is of high or low status? I do not care whether he is rich or poor, whether he is noble or lowly. You know very well that I will never marry someone who does not believe in the words of Jesus Christ, don't you?" How strange it feels, to think that I will soon be married.

⁚ Ewha Haktang Middle School's first commencement ceremony (1908).

The conflicts and torments of a girl who had been nurturing big dreams built upon faith and knowledge but now against the walls of convention—a whole new set of conflicts that earlier generations of women never before faced.

Ever since the school's earliest years, Ewha's students had been heightening their sense of responsibility as pioneers, through prayer and meditation. A widely quoted anecdote portrays Dr. Helen Kim, who later became the first Korean and first Ewha alumna to be appointed as the university's president, as a young, fun-loving girl awakening to her calling when she heard, during prayer, a voice from the Heavens calling out to her, "Do you hear it, the outcry of Korean women? How can you sit there if you have heard this?" To never marry and devote their lives to those in need was the future that Ewha students pictured for themselves.

Principal Rothweiler was clear in the educational vision she had for Ewha, that the school aimed at "making Koreans better Koreans," not "turning Koreans into foreigners."

> The goal of our education lies in assisting Korean women to build and maintain families, and to become teachers at our school, assistants at our dormitories, and nurses at our clinic… (Our students) must learn to prepare food and make clothing and keep their bodies and homes clean. All

> these must be done the Korean way... and we must teach them according to Korean systems, ensuring that they are not alienated from their fellow Koreans, and that they do not harbor discontent about their environment.

The missionaries' educational ideology helped Ewha take firm root in Korean soil. The girls of this country, who did not even own proper Korean names, were given Christian names like Lucy, Emma and Esther, and took on the role as pioneers in Korea's early days of modernization as they moved forward on the paths to humane lives based on the Christian spirit.

Ewha Haktang proudly takes up the first page in the history of women's education in Korea. The founding of Ewha created a whole new social class—that of schoolgirls cultivated by formal education. Ewha shook up the traditional rules of gender and launched a new history of change and potential.

1910

1925

Ⅱ

The College at Ewha Haktang

Confronting Challenges

: Emerson Chapel

Competing with Men

Since Ewha set out to carry the torch in the cause for women's education in Korea, the kingdom of Joseon began to see more and more girls heading to school, their traditional head dress taken off, carrying book bundles strapped to their backs. Schools served as a fountain of knowledge for the girls who had been thirsty for education. Once they experienced the joy of learning, there was no stopping them.

The students at Ewha naturally began to seek higher education upon completing the middle school curriculum. A college-level education was in demand and the school was also in urgent need of formally trained Korean teachers.

Since her early days in office, Ewha's fourth principal Lulu E. Frey had been envisioning the establishment of an institution offering higher education for women. In an article titled "Higher Education for Korean Girls," Principal Frey expressed regret regarding the custom of early marriage in Korea, which pulled students who were mentally and physically immature out of school:

> It has been said that the duration of childhood is extended with the advancement of civilization. One of the biggest reasons for establishing a higher education program at our school is to extend our students' time in enrollment, thereby helping the girls achieve further mental, emotional and physical maturity and stability.

Frey's plans, however, faced immediate opposition. It was a time when opening higher education institutions in this country, which had fallen under Japanese occupation, was a difficult endeavor. The colonial government had promulgated the Private School Decree in 1908, which served as the legal apparatus for controlling Korea's education system, vital to their agenda toward obliterating Korean culture and sovereignty. The act interfered with the execution of higher education in the country by setting strict limitations on school permits, curriculum and teacher qualifications, with an aim to deter the cultivation of new national leaders.

Lulu E. Frey, the 4th Principal, established the College at Ewha Haktang.

This was not the only obstacle that Frey had to overcome. When it came to higher education for women, not only parents and the general public but the missionaries believed it was too radical an idea. It was socially unacceptable that a woman continued to attend school past the marriageable age of 20.

Frey, however, carried a personal commitment to the cause of women's higher education that was more urgent than any ideology: She considered herself a chronicler of the narrative of women's development in Korea. Serving as Ewha's principal, she had witnessed first-hand the painful experiences of the country's women, and had seen in their eyes despair, hope, and a thirst "that will never be satisfied until they are in a position to compete side by side with men." This had led her to advocate the necessity of higher education for women, emphasizing that "the future of this country depends on its women," and worked towards her goal of cultivating the women of this country under the banner of Christian-spirited higher education, in order to build a strong workforce and produce competent leaders.

The College at Ewha Haktang opened its doors in the spring of 1910, by upgrading the middle school curriculum and reorganizing its high school courses. Considering that even in the U.S., a college for women was first established in the 1800s, it was a near miracle that one had opened in Korea, where women's education was still a new concept. A miracle that would never have been possible had it not been for the faith and determination of Principal Frey, who had overcome Japanese colonial oppression and public opposition.

The College's First Years

The College finally opened after a long period of struggle and waiting, but there remained many urgent problems that needed to be addressed, including curriculum review, faculty recruitment, and improvement and expansion of facilities. Fifteen students enrolled in its first year, most of them graduates of Ewha's middle or high school program and also a few who had returned from studying in Japan and other countries. Enhancing the quality of the educational environment was vital to meeting the expectation of the students and to providing them with a professional education.

Principal Frey submitted a request to the headquarters of the Woman's Foreign Missionary Society for additional faculty while locally recruiting qualified new teachers, which allowed

The faculty of the College at Ewha Haktang during its early years.

her to offer new courses at the College. Hah Ran-sa was one of many Ewha Haktang graduates who joined the faculty at this time. Hah, the aforementioned married woman who had visited Ewha Haktang in the middle of the night to demand a chance to learn and helped shape Frey's grand vision of higher education for Korean women, had now returned as her former teacher's colleague.

Other Ewha Haktang alumnae who took up teaching at the College after studying overseas included Lee Eun-ra, Helen Choi, Alice Kim, Park In-duk and Helen Kim. Standing side by side with the missionaries, dressed in sophisticated suits, these Korean women served as role models for the students. Among them, some, like Hah, went on to commit their lives to the cause of Korea's independence movement, while some, like Lee Eun-ra, devoted decades of service at Ewha.

Male faculty was very rare at the time. One was Professor Lee Seong-hoe, who started out as a teacher of Chinese characters at Ewha Haktang, and his responsibility also included dressing up as Santa Claus and distributing Christmas presents to students. His legacy was such that after he left Ewha, they were unable to find someone to fill his shoes at Christmas and the women faculty resorted to hiding behind a curtain in the auditorium to give out presents with a fishing hook. Considering that up to the 1920s in Korea 90% of those in the teaching

Hah Ran-sa, the first Korean student to pursue a degree in the U.S.

profession were men, Ewha was a radical exception.

Even though the College was equipped with specialized faculty, its students received a broad liberal arts education, without declaring a specific major. This allowed the Korean girls, who had limited exposure to modern knowledge, access to a wide range of disciplines including geography, astronomy, mathematics, pedagogy, ethics and psychology. Ewha placed emphasis on the teaching of English, music and athletics. The students were required to spend a significant number of class hours participating in physical education to keep healthy and to seek a balance between the development of mind and body.

It was no easy feat, however, to teach the girls to move their bodies and to learn the rules of sports games in the school's early days. They had not been encouraged to engage in uninhibited physical activity, and the kind of movements required to play Western athletics like basketball, tennis, volleyball, baseball and gymnastics proved awkward and embarrassing for them. Since they were unfamiliar with the concept of sportsmanship, there were also students who had difficulty accepting defeat, demanding that the game go on beyond conclusion. Physical education classes offered a chance not only for physical development but for reforming old customs and conventions as well.

The College also gained wide recognition for its cultural activities, including the Christian rituals at Easter and Christmas, and many school festivities, from picnics and theater performances to concerts and stage productions, which introduced a whole new youth culture to Korea. Ewha's anniversary celebrations that took place on the last day of May were the highlight of the year, with huge crowds from around the city gathering at the Jeong-dong campus to participate in a rich array of programs that included mass games and the May Queen coronation ceremony.

Student population multiplied as the College's outstanding education programs began earning recognition, and facility expansion emerged as the most immediate task at hand as classes had been taking place in crammed corners of the missionaries' living quarters. The school purchased the run-down Sontag Hotel and carried out partial repairs and renovations, but this was not enough to accommodate the increasing number of students. This left the faculty without much choice but to design a new building on their own, which resulted in the construction of Frey Hall. The building exclusively housed the College, including dormitory, classrooms and library, equipped with modern facilities including electricity, plumbing and heating.

Over 2,000 guests attended the dedication ceremony for

: Frey Hall exclusively housed the College at Ewha Haktang.

: The Library at Frey Hall.

Frey Hall in 1923. Named after the College's founder, the new hall carried far more meaning than that of a mere building: It was a symbol of the advancements achieved in women's education and at the same time a blueprint of Ewha's future.

Leading New Trends in Fashion

A. Jeannette Walter and Olive F. Pye, two teachers at Ewha Haktang, noticed one day during P.E. class their students stopping to readjust their traditional *hanbok* while immersed in the game. Comprised of a short blouse and a long strapless skirt that sat above the chest, and worn with layers of multiple undergarments, *hanbok* created an elegant silhouette but was not suited for physical activity.

Walter and her fellow missionaries grappled with the issue of improving the function of the traditional dress, and came up with a new design comprising a longer shirt and a reformed skirt with a vest attached to add comfort and practicality. This gym skirt would be an important turning point in the history of Korean clothing. Many students rejected the change when it was first introduced, breaking into tears when they were handed out patterns in sewing class to remodel the skirts that their mothers had made for them. As they experienced first-hand the practicality of the new skirt, however, news began to spread and soon the Ewha-style gym skirt gained popularity around the country.

Since this breakthrough change, Ewha began to lead the movement to update *hanbok* for modern times. In the 1950s, when Western attire became the dominant trend, there were many women professors at Ewha who continued to dress in new versions of *hanbok*, showing off their graceful silhouettes and colors on the campus.

Having been exposed to Western culture through faculty who had come from or studied overseas, the women of Ewha served as leaders of fashion trends in Korea. It was Helen Choi, an Ewha Haktang alumna, who in the 1920s introduced the *hanbok*-style white-shirt-and-black-skirt and the pompadour hairdo, which came to define the "modern girl' look of 1920s Korea.

When Choi returned to Korea in 1907 after studying in Tokyo, she had walked off the ship wearing a short skirt with ankle socks and leather pumps, her hair worn up in *hisashigami* style, the popular Japanese version of the pompadour. This style spread at great speed among young Korean stu-

A. Jeannette Walter's gymnastics class in the 1910s.

dents, referred to as the "cow dung hairdo" or the "twist-bun hairdo."

The highlight of Korean fashion innovation in the 1920s and 30s was the bob cut, also initiated by an Ewha graduate and faculty, Dr. Helen Kim. She was headed to Europe in 1928 to attend an academic conference when, during a stopover at Saigon Port in Vietnam, she noticed long-haired Chinese dockworkers and how their hair was an inconvenience in doing their work. She decided there and then that she would wear her hair short for the cause of progress and development. As soon as the ship reached Marseille, the next port of call, she had her long locks cut in a bob style.

It was a time in Korea's early modern years when women's hair and fashion were a constant source of controversy, and the bob cut received strong criticism for destroying the pure refined beauty of Joseon women. Dr. Kim spoke out in defense of the new style, asserting that it was no different from "clipping one's nails or washing one's hands," and that opposing this change was to adhere to outmoded conventions. There had been women before her who had endorsed the new style, but Helen Kim's bob cut became the center of public attention, gaining recognition as the new look of Korea's progressive-minded women.

These new styles, introduced to the public as "Ewha fash-

: The College's students in their fashionable pompadours.

: Students of the Middle School and the College at Ewha Haktang (1912).

ion," continued to lead trends and defined the look of the school girl, a whole new social status in Korea's early modern years.

First-Generation Women Leaders

On a spring day in 1914, when pear blossoms were abloom, a group of guests gathered at the Chungdong First Methodist Church. Inside the chapel, all of Ewha Haktang's students were lined up, dressed in the formal white *hanbok*. When three young women walked in, clad in black gowns and caps, guests and students all rose and offered a round of heart-felt applause. It was a historical moment in the commencement ceremony for Korea's first women college graduates. The air inside the chapel was swelling with excitement and emotion.

The first graduates of the College at Ewha Haktang were Alice Kim, Marcella Shin and Dorothy Lee, three among the 15 women who had entered the College's inaugural freshman class. At the special worship service held the previous day to commemorate the commencement, the three women had presented talks on their graduation theses, respectively titled, "Play as Education Element," "A Study of Korean Art," and "American Poet Henry Wadsworth Longfellow." The breadth of their research topics, and the fact that the talks were given in both Korean and English, speak for the high level of education at Ewha.

Considering the wide-spread practice of early marriage in Korea at the time, college education was a great privilege for women, and at the same time a source of envy and misconception. The status of a school girl was still a controversial one, and college women often became the center of public attention, usually on a negative note, for wasting time for the sake of intellectual vanity.

Tuition was also an issue in women's higher education. According to statistics, tuition ranked as the biggest obstacle in students pursuing or continuing education in Joseon at the time. Many households were in dire financial states and could not afford to pay tuition. In order to help students stay in school, Ewha introduced a financial aid plan. College students could receive a tuition waiver on the condition that they serve on the school's faculty upon graduation, which also proved to be an effective way to encourage female students to maintain a career.

The women of Ewha possessed great pride in their status as educated elites, all the more for the hardships that they had to face in their pursuit of higher education. Their pride also instilled in them a sense of social responsibility, which is evident in the contributions made by Ewha alumnae as women leaders and pioneers.

During its early years, the College at Ewha Haktang produced Korea's first generation of professional women who went overseas to acquire advanced degrees. Beginning with Helen Kim, who upon completing her dissertation in philosophy at Columbia University became the first Korean woman to earn a Ph.D., a string of Ewha alumnae received recognition in their fields of specialization and assumed leader roles: Helen Choi and Park In-duk were active in women's movement and religious organizations; Esther Hwang founded the Pine and Bamboo Society, one of the first women's organizations devoted to Korea's independence movement, and made a mark in the cause for the enlightenment of women and rural communities; and Kim Won-ju, also known as penname Ilyeop, was an author who belonged to Korea's first-generation of women writers.

The number of college-educated women was extremely small at the time, and even among them, a majority settled down as housewife after graduation, which adds further promi-

The first commencement ceremony at the College at Ewha Haktang
—Marcella Shin, Dorothy Lee and Alice Kim (1914).

nence to the achievements of the Ewha alumnae.

Their social accomplishments had been fueled by student activity at Ewha, which encouraged its students to form various societies and clubs promoting religious activity or volunteer work. For students enrolled in the College, these extracurricular activities were compulsory.

Ewha's many clubs included the Literary Society, King's Daughters, the Missionary Society, the Purity League, the Ewha Seven Member Evangelical Mission and the Ewha YWCA. The Literary Society was widely known for its weekly gatherings, which included heated debates on a range of topics. Its members organized lectures by renowned speakers and music or theater performances. Their debates drew crowds of students who filled the auditorium.

The rest were mostly worship clubs that promoted not merely individual spiritual development but social volunteer work rooted in the Christian spirit of neighborly love, which under colonial rule expanded into the save-the-nation movement. The Ewha Seven Member Evangelical Mission is a good example, established in the summer of 1919, a few months after the March 1 Independence Movement, by six students who planned a cross-country evangelism tour with Dr. Helen Kim as head of the mission. They hoped to uphold Ewha founder Mary F. Scranton's sense of mission, to bring the Christian

The College's Literary Society.

King's Daughters, an evangelical student club at Ewha.

gospel to those suffering from poverty and ignorance. Leaving Seoul to visit various corners of the country, they embarked on a miraculous journey that grew into a rural enlightenment movement in alliance with local youth organizations, invigorating remote communities by offering hope and assistance. The mission emerged as an influential group whose visits alerted the Japanese colonial police force.

It is not difficult to find among the member lists of Ewha's clubs names of women who went on to become prominent leaders in society. The clubs served as incubators where their training in leadership first began.

Ewha continued to make history in women's development in the face of colonial oppression and conventions of sexual discrimination. The role that women leaders from Ewha played in society spoke for the significance and importance of Ewha's goal to produce educated women elites.

⁚ The Ewha Seven Member Evangelical Mission led at the forefront of the rural enlightment campaign.

1925

1945

III

Ewha College

Half-Century of Miracles

: Pfeiffer Hall (Main Hall)

Truth, Goodness and Beauty —Spirit of Harmony and Balance

Korean school girls in the 1920s and 30s were marked not only by their modernized black skirts and leather pumps, but the school badges pinned to their chests. When a series of felony cases involving young men and women posing as students drew public attention, schools came up with ways to provide student identification and to strengthen a sense of identity, including school badges and anthems.

It was around 1930 that Ewha established its university identity, including symbol, slogan, badge and anthem. On April 23, 1925, the College and the College Preparatory Program at Ewha Haktang had been reorganized into a single entity as the Ewha College and received government accreditation as a professional school, offering specialized education in a range of disciplines.

Ewha's anthem conveyed the school's high ideals and spirit in a dignified 4/4 time marching tune, with lyrics written by the revered historian Chung In-bo. Comprised of three verses, the song narrates the history of Ewha as a pioneer of women's history and modernization in Korea:

We bloom by Han River in the warm spring breeze,
And the holy one hath called it Ewha, oh Ewha.
We sing out holy songs sweetly and softly.
The Kingdom of Heaven is here in our midst.

We yearn for the true spirit of honor and virtue.
Shown by our great women.
'Tis a guide to us all.
We are gathered here to grow, learn, and strive.
And wrap the whole land in our virtue and grace.

Stand tall, and reach for the sky with our high spirit.
Our duty is always to reach out.
Let no one go astray.
Like the Lord is always around us watching,
Stand in awe of God,
God's light shines on us.

Ewha, Ewha, our Ewha!

True, good and beautiful Ewha.
Spread your sweet scent far and wide.
Ah, our Ewha.

As reflected in the anthem, Ewha's educational vision of cultivating wholesome students armed with intellect, virtue and sensibility is represented by the three keywords—truth, goodness and beauty.

The design motif for the school emblem was the pear blossom, signifying purity and abundant fruits. Wearing this symbol on their chests provided Ewha's students with a unique sense of identity distinguishable from other schools.

This vision of balance and harmony was central to education at Ewha. Following accreditation, the school was restructured into two separate systems, the Ewha College and the Ewha Training School for Early Education: The former was divided into three departments, literary, music and home economics, while the latter was expanded from the College's early education department, the first of its kind in Korea. The College and the Training School soon emerged as the most prominent breeding grounds for pioneers in each discipline.

It is notable that physical education was considered the most important of all liberal arts courses offered at Ewha, a means of practicing balance and harmony and seeking the development of both mind and body. Athletic activity at the school had received much public attention since the early days of Ewha Haktang, for in Korea it was still a source of debate and sensation, the sight of girls of marriageable age running around in their athletic uniforms—white blouse and black bloomers—learning gymnastics and modern dance, participating in softball or badminton matches. Soon magazines and newspapers began to feature images of women dressed in athletic wear that revealed their curves, engaged in sports activity. Thanks to Ewha's physical education, the requirements of a cultivated modern woman came to include leisure sports in addition to sophisticated musical hobbies like piano playing.

Similar standards applied to Ewha's Posture Queen Contest, held as part of the annual Fall Field Day festivities, launched after the Japanese colonial government closed down the May Queen Contest. The criteria for selecting the Posture Queen had less to do with appearance but with spiritual purity and a healthy body achieved through exercise and discipline. In order to be selected, students practiced good walking habits and upright bearing, which made them easily distinguishable even on the streets.

Everything that the Ewha students did became the talk of the town as they gained recognition as icons of liberation from conventions and restrictions.

: Posture Queen Contest.

P.E. class in the gymnasium.

The Ewha Girl: High Ideals, Classy Style

"Ewha is heaven for women."
"At Ewha, all Koreans, including teachers, communicate only in Korean and not Japanese."
"At Ewha, you can learn to speak fluent English."
"Every Ewha graduate is a skilled piano player."

An air of confidence and pride reflected in their classy, clean-cut styles was what set the Ewha College students apart, receiving from other young women both admiration and envy for their sophisticated tastes and liberal attitude. At the same time, they also became targets of criticism from men.

During the 1920s and 1930s, several newspapers and magazines carried feature articles that highlighted the different characteristics of various women's colleges, which included a piece titled, "Commentary on College Women as Categorized by School (*New Women*, May 1926)," and a survey of male college students on school girls (*Eastern Light*, 1932). In these articles, the girls at Ewha High School and Ewha College are depicted using expressions like "high collar," which was a term referring to a sophisticated look, along with "extravagant," "arrogant," "in Western skin," "merry in spirit," and "American-style." It is interesting that in contrast, other neighboring women's schools like Sookmyung, Jinmyeong and Dongduk were viewed as "gentle," "modest," "disciplined" and "prudish."

The public came to refer to Ewha's students as "Ewha girls," using the English word instead of Korean, to highlight the fact that these students were accustomed to Western lifestyles, sleeping in beds and not on floor beddings, taking their meals at dining tables, not low tray-tables. The irony was that the missionaries' efforts to provide a Western education and lifestyle for abandoned and neglected girls had resulted in a public image of these girls as privileged connoisseurs of Western culture. The curiosity and envy of men, unfamiliar with Western lifestyles, turned into outright malicious accusations that the girls were "of bad breeding, influenced by American culture, prone to extravagance and putting on airs that smelled of butter." The term "Ewha girl," in other words, projected the contradictory

Students of Ewha.

attitudes of Korean men towards modern women and school girls, veering from admiration to rejection, from envy to insecurity. One thing seems clear however, that Ewha College students were considered to possess high ideals, a vibrant spirit and classy style.

Treasury of the Modern, Romantic Spirit

Ewha's image as a symbol of Western modernity was not a groundless one. The school's campus was like a foreign country in the middle of Joseon, its buildings equipped with state-of-the-art facilities that provided students with an experience of advanced lifestyles including window curtains, electric lighting, central heating, and flush toilets. The fact that the school grounds were a no-man's land, accessible only to women, elevated public curiosity and suspicion, spinning myriad speculations and rumors.

In Ewha's dorms, students from around the country shared rooms, four girls assigned to each room. Some students commuted from their homes in Seoul, but it was a tradition that goes back to the school's Ewha Haktang days to encourage stu-

Hwanghwasa, the dormitory's new annex.

dents to experience communal living in the dorms.

In Korea at the time, college girls living in boarding houses away from home were perceived as disreputable women who pursued a loose lifestyle, which called for strict rules and order at the dormitories of women's colleges. Above a mirror in the doorway of Ewha's dormitory building hung a sign with the message, "Let all things be done decently and in order," which had been inlaid with mother-of-pearl during the Ewha Haktang years by then-housemother Hah Ran-sa.

Ewha's dormitories were operated by an autonomous governing body named Frey Hall Sister's Garden, which oversaw all routines and regulations: Mail was delivered not through the housemother but by a student staff member, and the students decided through vote all issues regarding dorm life, from menu and room conditions to daily rules. It was a system devised by the school as a means to nurture independence and self-rule in the students, preparing them for leadership in society.

Strict regulations ruled dorm life, but it was also a haven where memories of friendship and camaraderie were made. A strong sense of sisterhood was cultivated through a mentoring system called "Love Sisters" that paired freshmen with upperclassmen to assist them in adapting to new surroundings. The pairings were undisclosed and each couple established tight bonds, helping out with laundry and other chores, meeting in one another's rooms, pillows tucked at their sides, for long late-night conversations, organizing secret meetings at the dorm's attic where intimate tales were shared outside the watchful eyes of the teachers. In early November, the school took a special break so all of Ewha's students could participate in pickling *kimchi* for the coming winter, during which the upperclassmen would often unintentionally reveal their partners while trying to deliver *kimchi* wraps prepared for their freshmen sister.

When students returned to school at the beginning of each semester, the dormitory bustled with chatter and activity as the girls unpacked local delicacies that they had brought back from home, starting a small party in each room.

While school was in session, weekends were what the dorm residents looked most forward to, since individual outings were permitted on Saturdays, and on Sundays, the students attended service together at the Chungdong First Methodist Church. A typical Ewha girl's Saturday outing downtown started with an early-bird screening of French film at the Meiji Theater, followed by window shopping at Mitsukoshi Department Store and a stop at a used bookstore in the Honmachi neighborhood—an accurate depiction of a modern, urban intellectual's life in Seoul under Japanese colonial rule.

Ewha, Built on Love and Prayer

It was in 1935 that Ewha moved to its current campus in Sinchon. On March 9, Ewha President Alice R. Appenzeller left the Jeong-dong school building, carrying Mary Scranton's photo as she made her way along the ridge of Mt. Geumhwa and arrived at Pfeiffer Hall, the main building of the Sinchon campus. The beautiful white granite building with the green tile roof revealed itself in the spring sunlight, amidst the cherry blossoms and maidenhair trees. It was a historical day, of bringing the school's 50 years of achievements in Jeong-dong to this new site where Ewha's new future would unfold. Joyous hymns were sung, for a long period of longing had finally borne fruit.

President Appenzeller, who was appointed to office in 1922, had long envisioned the establishment of a full-scale uni-

⁚ Ewha students and faculty singing a hymn outside Pfeiffer Hall to celebrate the move to the new campus in 1935.

⁚ Pfeiffer Hall, the first building on the Sinchon campus.

versity and the construction of a new campus. There was great demand at the time for a women's university but the Joseon Education Decree, proclaimed by the Japanese colonial government, prohibited Koreans from pursuing education beyond college or professional school. This, however, did not deter Appenzeller from offering her desperate prayers for five years as she worked toward securing land in the Sinchon area and promoted her cause to seek funding from home and abroad.

In the fall of 1923, Helen Kim, Ewha-alumna-turned-faculty, attended the executive assembly of the Woman's Foreign Missionary Society held in Des Moines, Iowa, where she donated the brass bell from Ewha Haktang to solicit aid for the school. Kim had rung this bell every day during her years as student at Ewha Haktang, a job that she had taken on in return for tuition support. She presented this bell to the society with a prayer-like letter:

> I hereby donate to Mrs. Nicholson for the museum of the Woman's Foreign Missionary Society, this bell from Ewha Haktang, which has awakened the women of Korea. The bell has been heard since the construction of the school's Main Hall, alerting the girls that it was time for them to wake up, to get to class, to take their meals, to attend service, to say their prayers… Today the bell is ringing again, together with the voices calling out in support of our plan

A drawing of the Sinchon campus.

> to build a university, and in need of 25,000 dollars... Yes, we the women of Korea are down on our knees, our hands joined in prayer and our heads raised upward, longing to be a part of your mission to lead the world to redemption. Please listen to the bell ring one more time. Again and again it rings, amidst a silence that is infinite.

Ewha's yearning to sow the seeds of learning that awoke the women of Korea and to bring fruition in the form of a university was delivered by the ringing of the bell to the women gathered in Des Moines that evening.

The ringing was answered, however, thousands of miles away, on Ewha's school grounds. A guest had come calling that day, a woman named Almena Studley Gray, in Korea to visit her son who was a missionary in Korea. The Canadian missionary Grace Saxe had recommended that she pay a call to Ewha, and the school's administrators guided her to the new campus site in Sinchon. On this rainy winter day, the vast grounds appeared to be a land of promise and miracles. Could it be that Gray saw that day the future of Ewha, surrounded by an air of hope? She decided, on the spot, that she would make a donation, and upon returning to the U.S., sent 30,000 dollars to be spent on land purchase and construction.

Fundraising efforts for the Sinchon campus drew attention

from a wide range of potential donors. Mr. and Mrs. Henry G. Pfeiffer were among the many people from different parts of the world who had sent money. The couple were devout Methodists and philanthropists who had been donating large amounts of business profits to education and religious and social causes in many countries. Upon hearing President Appenzeller's desperate plea, they offered funding for the construction of the main hall of a school in a faraway country they had never been to, thereby making an important contribution to the making of the Sinchon campus.

At the last chapel service before the move to Sinchon, President Appenzeller announced, moved with emotion, "Our Ewha is the crystallization of numerous people's prayers and love. There is no one person that built Ewha: Ewha was born from the love of many throughout the world."

In the Hands of an Ewha-Educated Korean

The history of Ewha was built upon the foundation of one American missionary's dedication, its growth achieved by the dream and hope from supporters around the world. However, as Ewha's role and reputation within the Korean society grew more significant, there was increasing demand for its independence, that the country's most prestigious educational institution for women should not be left in the hands of foreigners.

In response to this public opinion, leading dignitaries organized the Ewha College Support Committee in 1932, under the slogan, "From Management by the Church to Management by Society." This committee served as the cornerstone for the Ewha Haktang Foundation, which provided the basis for Ewha's independence, leading the shift from a school run by the Woman's Foreign Missionary Society to a Korean college run by Koreans.

The appointment of alumna Helen Kim as Ewha's president was a major turning point that publicly declared Ewha's determination in its pursuit of independence. Kim was the first Korean woman to earn a Ph.D., who, upon returning from her studies in philosophy at Columbia University, joined the Ewha faculty before taking office as Ewha College's first Korean president in 1939. She went on to serve as the first president of Ewha Womans University, gaining international recognition as a prominent scholar in the fields of women's education, politics and diplomacy, and Christian studies. She was in many ways a symbol of Ewha, raised and shaped by the school. It was clear she was the best candidate for carrying out President Appenzeller's vision that Ewha must be managed in the hands of a Korean, one who has been educated at Ewha.

It was a time when Japanese colonial oppression of the Christian church and missionary schools was growing harsher. Ewha struggled to keep the school open, relenting to the coercion to worship at Japanese *shinto* shrines following the Methodist church's decision, but the persecution of missionaries continued to intensify. After tense confrontation with the colonial government, President Appenzeller and other missionaries withdrew from Korea, bidding farewell to Ewha after a lifetime

: Helen Kim with outgoing president Appenzeller on Kim's inauguration as Ewha's first Korean president (1939).

Students bid farewell to missionaries departing Korea (1940).

of service.

Left on its own after the departure of the missionaries, the Ewha community prepared for the school's next leap forward, seeking hope in the face of anger and despair. In the end, the withdrawal of the missionaries presented a great ordeal for Ewha but at the same time an opportunity for seeking independence and further growth.

1945

1961

IV
Ewha Womans University

Standing Tall
in the Face of Hardship

Welch-Ryang Auditorium

The Dilemma of Coeducation

Under the harsh oppression of Japanese colonial rule during the 1940s, Ewha managed to preserve itself without letting go of its sense of duty as a pioneer in women's education despite the pressures and hardships it faced, which had resulted in the reorganization of the curriculum at Ewha College and the change of its name. Many other schools had been downsized or closed down, but the Ewha community was determined to keep the school going, for upholding Ewha attested to the pride they possessed as Koreans and as women.

When these ordeals came to an end in 1945 with Korea's liberation, Ewha submitted an application to establish a formal university before any other school and in 1946 Ewha Womans University was officially accredited by the government as the first university in Korea. Accreditation reaffirmed Ewha's achievements in education and its status in the history of education in Korea. Over 1,000 students applied for university admission to Ewha, an impressive testimony of what Ewha had inspired in the hearts of Korean women throughout its 60 years of education.

As an accredited university, Ewha revised its statutes and upgraded its curriculum. Additional faculty was recruited and the library was expanded. The school was reorganized into three separate colleges: the College of Liberal Arts (Literary, Home Economics, Education, and Physical Education Departments); the College of Fine Arts (Departments of Music and Fine Arts); and the College of Healing Arts (Departments of Pharmacy and Medicine). It was also during this period that the university's teaching hospital and the university press opened. Most notable was the establishment of the graduate school in March of 1950, which reaffirmed Ewha's position as a research university and an incubator for Korea's foremost women leaders.

Ewha was undoubtedly the center of women's education in Korea, but there were talks at one point to shift to coeducation. There had been speculations from time to time, and in 1946 administrators from Seoul's three major Christian schools, Ewha, Yonhi and Severance, met to discuss closer cooperation,

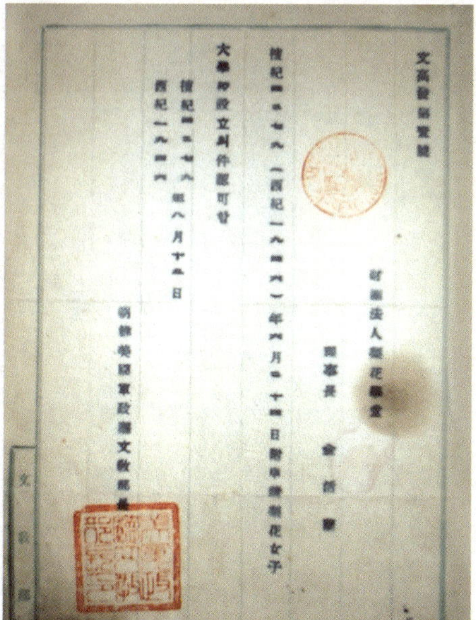

Ewha becomes first university in Korea to receive government accreditation (1946).

Students on Ewha's Sinchon campus.

which continued as an regular gathering for the next three years, and as a result, Yonhi and Severance merged, becoming Yonsei University. At the talks, Ewha agreed to the proposal to share school buildings and facilities, but made it clear that it had a mission to uphold as a women's education institution, which set it apart from the other schools.

The prospect of Ewha offering coeducation continued to be a subject of debate in the decades that followed. On March 11, 1971, the national daily *Chosun Ilbo* broke news that Ewha was considering accepting male students, which incited inquiries from alumnae and phone calls protesting, "Whoever is discussing the possibility of going coed, kick this person out." On another occasion, a reporter asked President Helen Kim when Ewha planned to go coed and Kim replied, "When all sexual discrimination has been abolished in Korea, with equal numbers of male and female representatives in the National Assembly."

Nevertheless, advocates of coeducation at Ewha have continued to raise their voices over the years. In the 1970s, the Ewha Development Research Committee for New Decade carried out a careful examination of the choice between women's education and coeducation, and in the 1980s, the university paper the *Ewha Weekly* ran a special feature titled, "If Ewha Goes Coed." In each instance, Ewha's leadership have been consistent in their response that the school was founded to carry out the mission of women's education in Korea, and that it would remain a sanctuary for women.

Pursuing Dreams in Times of War

One day in January 1951, at the height of the Korean War, an advertisement was published in papers under the heading, "Calling Ewha's Faculty." Upon seeing the ad, the school's professors and students, who had fled the war to different parts of the country, began to gather, one by one, at Ewha's newly opened wartime evacuee campus in the southern port of Busan, harboring hope and anticipation. It was seven months after the school had closed down on June 27, 1950, upon the outbreak of war.

At the time, the Ministry of Culture and Education was operating a joint wartime university program, but Ewha decided to run its own separate program, an audacious attempt in those war-torn times. A total of 859 students enrolled in

Ewha's evacuee program, which spoke for the students' thirst for education.

Their zeal for learning remained strong despite the lack of supplies and the poor conditions at the makeshift facilities. During its years in Busan, Ewha launched its first academic journal, *Educational Research*, and became Korea's first private university to establish a teacher's college. Such achievements were possible thanks to overseas supporters like Friends of Ewha, who sent relief supplies for the school.

On August 31, 1953, following an armistice agreement between South and North Koreas, Ewha finally returned to Seoul. But what awaited on the Sinchon campus was nothing less than devastating as the destroyed buildings reflected the wounds of war: Pfeiffer Hall stood with its roof blown away and its interior exposed; Wichita House, which had been under construction to serve as the president's residence, was torn down; the Home Management House burned down to ashes. The most urgent task was to restore and repair the buildings so that classes could resume. The school established a three-stage restoration plan that included repairs, expansions and new constructions, and got to work. It was during this period that Appenzeller Hall, Helen Hall, the old Student Union and the 4,000-seat Welch-Ryang Auditorium, the largest in Asia at the time, were constructed.

Throughout this period of restoration, classes went on uninterrupted, achieving new milestones in education. In 1954, Ewha conferred its first master's degrees to five students, a monumental accomplishment in the history of Korean education, especially considering the severe gender imbalance in learning opportunities. Commencement ceremony that year was a moving occasion that spoke for Ewha's determination to continue its education in the face of war and despair, turning hardship into an opportunity for further growth for its campus and in its academic pursuits.

May 31, 1956, was a truly special day as guests gathered to celebrate Ewha's 70th anniversary, with the entire student body attending in traditional white *hanbok* specially tailored for the ceremony, decorated with blue pear blossoms patterns and the name Ewha printed in English. The day's celebrations also included a dedication ceremony for the Welch-Ryang Auditorium. Standing tall atop a grand 45-step stairway, a magnificent cross carved in relief on its facade, the auditorium would become a new landmark on the Sinchon campus, serving as the center for worship and celebrations at Ewha. May Day festivities that year became the talk of the town, with a series of programs at the auditorium including a four-day run of "The Story of Chunhyang," a production participated by the College

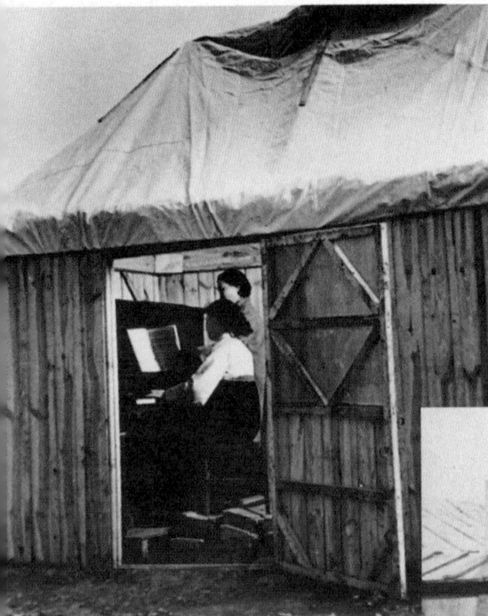

Music department classes taking place in tent facilities.

Ewha's evacuee campus in Busan during the Korean War (1951).

Overview of the Ewha campus during restorations following the war (1955).

of Academics' entire student body.

President Helen Kim's words spoke of the hope and vision that Ewha had brought amidst the war and its aftermath: "We shall not follow the flow of the times, the times shall follow us."

May Queen —Between Convention and Tradition

The highlight of the 70th anniversary celebrations was the May Queen Coronation Ceremony. The tradition dated back to 1908 when Ewha held its first official anniversary celebration, but had been held intermittently through colonial oppression and political chaos during the war, resuming in 1947 after nine years of absence.

In the beginning, the May Queen honor was awarded to a respected faculty member or alumna. It was in 1927 that the students began electing a senior student for the honor. Unlike conventional beauty contests, the selection criteria were based on the Ewha spirit of truth, goodness and beauty, with an emphasis not only on intellectual looks and sophisticated style but academic performance, character and religious faith.

May Queen Coronation Ceremony (1928).

The May Queen coronation kicked off with a march of the students, followed by the honoree in light blue *hanbok* taking the throne on center stage. The flower wreath crown was then presented by a student representative as the students sang "I Crown You Our Queen" amidst applause from the audience.

There was great public interest in the annual contest and the ceremony received heated coverage from the press despite the school's efforts to keep out journalists. Once during the Korean War, an unidentified woman in Busan created a stir after posing as a former May Queen, handing out notes autographed "MQ," which brought some damage to the contest's reputation.

While public fascination with the event grew, the May Queens being featured on the cover of magazines, there was increased criticism among the students that the contest was an outdated tradition rooted in a male-oriented culture, and an insult to womanhood. Some continued to uphold it as an important Ewha tradition, but as the contest turned more commercial, student opinion began to gear toward the negative. Student participation in the event began to drop and surveys showed that a majority of students supported abolishing the contest. The school made the official decision to close down the contest following the last coronation ceremony in 1977.

The May Queen Contest had started out with the purpose

Ewha's 70th anniversary commemoration ceremony (1956).

of honoring role models for women in the early days of Ewha when educated women were a rarity. During the Ewha College years, many May Queen honorees went on to become dedicated and socially responsible professionals in the fields of education and women's movement.

Today the May Queen wreath crown is on display at Ewha as the legacy that it once held in public spotlight.

Bringing Light to the Deserts of Pakistan

Early one morning in November of 1961, three young women got off the plane at Karachi International Airport. They were Jo Seong-ja, Jeon Jae-ok and Kim Eun-ja, recent graduates of Ewha Womans University. They had arrived here with a historical task as the first overseas missionaries in the history of the Christian church in Korea. Their trip from Seoul's Kimpo International Airport had taken six days, after one year and three months of delay as travel plans stalled, but they had now finally landed on this unfamiliar land, filled with excitement, curiosity and fear. Greeting them at the airport with a big, generous smile was Bishop Chandu Ray of the Karachi Diocese.

This encounter had been arranged by Bishop Ray's proposal to President Helen Kim to dispatch missionaries to Pakistan, submitted upon hearing news of a revival meeting at the Ewha Womans University Church. In 1960, Ewha had been actively expanding its revival and evangelist activities through the University Church and the Geumran Evangelistic Association. The two organizations' revival meetings were combined into joint efforts with other Methodist schools in Seoul, eventually turning into annual events of unprecedented scale.

Geumran Evangelistic Association was conceived by President Helen Kim, who had participated in a Bible reading group since 1953 while supervising an adult Bible study group at the University Church, which was expanded into an organization for mission work and enlightenment campaigns.

All mission work at the association was self-supported, and included rural volunteer work, medical missions to remote villages, and prayer groups and lectures to nurture the faith of its members. A proposal was made in July 1964 for the construction of the Upper Room. The name was taken in reference of the Cenacle from the early days of Christianity and the space served as a venue for the association's meetings, prayer, studies and projects, leading to a change in the association's name in 1966 to the Upper Room Evangelistic Association. It produced numerous leaders of the Christian church and contributed to the Christian movement in Korea as the birthplace of the national campaign to spread the gospel throughout Korea.

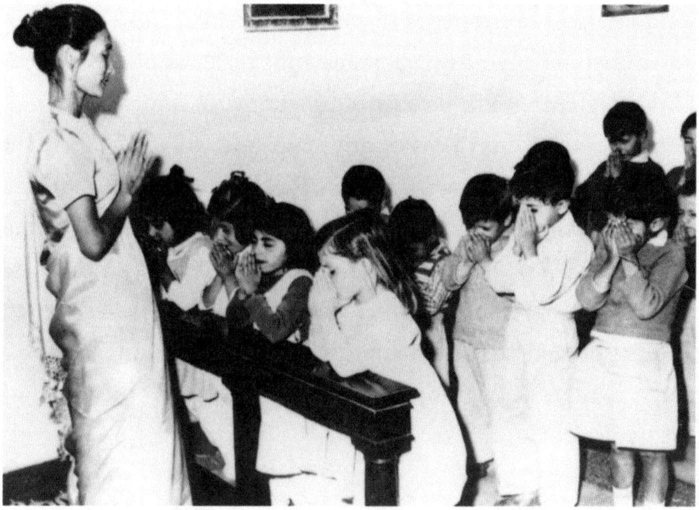

Ewha dispatched Korea's first missionaries to Pakistan (1961).

The three missionaries dispatched to Pakistan in 1961 devoted themselves to education and mission work at the Theresa Girls' High School in the city of Quetta, with spiritual and material support from the association and the University Church, which continued until 1973. The Student Council had provided support for the mission work, offering funding for the activities and prayers in times of dispute in the region. The association's successful mission was an important achievement, which showed that Ewha, once the beneficiary of mission work, had grown mature enough to give back to other parts of the world what it had received.

: The Upper Room.

1961

1979

V

Progress and Growth

Establishment of
Academic Tradition

: Main Gate

Commitment to Continue Onward

The year 1961 marked a major turning point in Ewha's passage of growth toward new developments and academic pursuits. It was also a time when the Korean society faced new challenges in the course of modernization, with the outbreak of the April 19 Revolution staged by student activists in 1960 and the May 16 coup d'etat in 1961 that brought an end to the wave of democratization and launched a military dictatorship. The social turmoil brought about unrest on university campuses around the country and Ewha was no exception.

Upon taking power in 1961, the new military regime proclaimed the University Restructuring Law, attempting to exert more control on schools and their students. The law included a clause that set the retirement age of faculty members at 60, which in effect forced President Helen Kim out of office. She was succeeded by theology scholar and women's leader Kim Okgill. The outgoing president, however, showed no signs of discouragement in the face of this sudden move by the new government, simply responding, "Well, I guess that means I've been sacked!" It was a move that she had seen coming and for the past two years she had been considering resigning.

> The best is yet to be; The last of life, for which the first was made.

President Helen Kim left office on September 30, 1961, after delivering a speech addressing her hope and anticipation for Ewha's future, closing with this line from a poem by Robert Browning. The farewell ceremony was covered extensively by the national press, celebrating the achievements of the "global Helen Kim" and her unyielding spirit.

Kim continued to serve Ewha as the President of the Ewha Haktang Foundation, traveling to the U.S. to raise funds for the establishment of the International Foundation for Ewha Womans University. She spent her last years dedicated to mission work, her life's cause, but was stricken with cerebral hemorrhage which took her life in February of 1970. In accordance with her will, a memorial service was held in the place of a

Inauguration ceremony for Ewha's 8th President Kim Okgill (1961).

funeral, with Verdi's "Grand March" played instead of a hymn, and a poem recited instead of a eulogy. In the words of the poet Mo Yun-suk, Helen Kim was Ewha's living history, who had "lifted herself up to liberate the women of this country from ignorance" and "given birth, amidst dark times, to eternal Ewha."

Incoming president Kim Okgill pledged in her inaugural speech to "move forward without turning back, armed with continuing dedication."

> We have a new captain on board but the boat is the same one. The same map, the same compass. The destination we are headed toward will not change. I have been on this boat through stormy waters and through calm. I shall continue to remain on it, bound by a common destiny.

After declaring that she would push forward as the captain in charge of Ewha's journey ahead, President Kim Okgill cropped her long hair, which she had worn up in her trademark Bible woman-style bun, into a short bob, and donned a handbag, whereas previously she had kept her hands pushed inside the pockets of her black traditional overcoat. This was when the clean-cut and graceful image of the bob-haired Ewha president was first created.

Ewha establishes Ten-Year Development Plan (1966).

Upon taking office, the new president focused her energy on making changes that would turn the school into a globalized institution. She pursued this goal firstly through increased international academic exchange to expand the worldviews of Koreans; and secondly, by developing a new system to promote research and establish new academic traditions. These two initiatives made up the core vision of Ewha's Ten-Year Development Plan, carried out between 1967 and 1976.

One of the biggest achievements made under President Kim's initiative was hosting the 1st General Meeting of Christian Women's Universities of Asia. Held at Ewha from May 23 to 31, 1972, this international conference was participated by nine women's university presidents from six countries to discuss the role of women's higher education in 21st-century Asia. The conference did not focus simply on diagnosing the current state of women's universities and the problems that entailed. Its significance lay in increasing solidarity between women's universities in a time that called for joint research by women in Asia, with an aim to humanize the lives of women as world citizens. Other accomplishments made at Ewha in internationalization and academic exchange include the new faculty exchange program; the international summer school; and graduate credit exchange between Ewha, Yonsei and Sogang Universities.

Building an Academic Tradition

The second goal in developing Ewha's stature as an international institution was to build a system to support the establishment of a strong academic tradition.

To achieve this goal, Ewha launched the Experimental University program, which allowed students to start university without declaring their major until the end of their freshman or sophomore year, earning credits in exploratory courses in the liberal arts. The program aimed at resolving chronic problems in higher education including imbalance between liberal arts and specialized courses and focus on self-interest among departments, and also at allowing more choice for students and more freedom in faculty research. At the time, high school seniors relied solely on their teachers in deciding their fields of study when applying for college, without much consideration of aptitude or potential. University departments, on their part, did not offer a flexible range of liberal arts and specialized courses, which led to dissatisfaction and discouragement in the students, many choosing to transfer to other majors.

The new exploratory program allowed students ample time to choose their major according to aptitude and career plans, diminishing the rate of misjudgment: In other words, the program aimed at not only supplementing the loopholes in the college admission process but also redeeming the university's stature and identity as an institution of higher education. Starting in 1973, applicants to Ewha's College of Liberal Arts were given a choice between the Humanities & Social Sciences Division and the Natural Sciences Division, declaring their majors in their sophomore or junior years, with additional choices to pursue a minor or a double major. The students were also given more autonomy in their academic routines, with reduced credit requirements.

While the program was created with high ideals, its execution posed several problems, the most evident of which was the heavy concentration of students in a handful of popular majors. In the College of Liberal Arts, the English Literature and Sociology Departments attracted several times their student capacity. There were also opinions that two years were insufficient for in-depth studies in their chosen disciplines. Some students complained of the changed academic atmosphere, lacking in commitment and sense of belonging. The faculty also admitted that there had been a lack of understanding about the program prior to its execution, and that perhaps the reforms were too radical.

The university invested much time in resolving the issues, seeking change in the program's operation for added flexibility, but in the end, faced with increasing opposition from students and faculty, decided to abolish it.

The Experimental University program was an innovative attempt at seeking a more effective university system, which did not guarantee quick success or rewards. It was only after a significant period of time that the program's vision and intent were reevaluated, in recognition of its validity. What was evident was that the program brought about a shift in the paradigm for innovation in the school system. The students were the first to admit that the exploratory program created a more liberal academic environment, where the students were faced with the responsibility of choice and free will, which in itself was at once a challenge and an accomplishment.

Fighting Political Oppression

In the period between the April 19 Revolution in 1960 and the military government's decision in 1965 to normalize ties with its former colonizer Japan, universities played a major role in the resistance against political oppression. The authoritarian regime took extraordinary measures to control student unrest, banning all types of autonomous student activity and launching the Students' Corps for National Protection, which in effect incorporated the entire university student population into a government-run organization. These measures, however, failed to quell student resistance, further igniting their struggle against the dictatorship.

Ewha's campus was also awash in the yearning for democracy and social justice. The students showed their devotion to the cause through protests, debates, lectures and performances being staged around campus every day.

The students' fervor culminated in a dramatic all-night prayer sit-in on November 28, 1973. Over 4,000 students and faculty had gathered at the Welch-Ryang Auditorium, the dreary early winter chill melting amidst the heated enthusiasm of their prayers. They denounced the government's crackdown on campus activity and called for democratization as they sang endless rounds of hymns and protest songs like "Pathfinder" and "Jesus of Golden Crown."

Earlier that afternoon, when mid-day chapel had come to a close at the auditorium, representatives of the Student Council took to the stage and recited a manifesto addressed to Ewha's 8,000 students, adopting six resolutions that included a call to end campus crackdown, amidst thunderous applause. The students marched out to the street, forming a scrum, and as the protest developed into a face-off with the police, many students were wounded and injured.

This was when President Kim decided to step forward. As injuries increased amidst tear gas bombs and physical confrontation with the police, Kim persuaded the students to turn back towards the auditorium. Student Council then had led the students to the auditorium for the sit-in.

The prayer vigil at Ewha reaffirmed what the university

President Kim Okgill standing at the head of the anti-dictatorship protest in 1973 to protect the students.

stood for, should work towards, and can accomplish in the Korean society, standing tall in unity and camaraderie in pursuit of a sustainable vision.

Romanticism of Youth Culture

Blue jeans, the guitar, draft beer, go-go dancing, folk music, long hair and miniskirts. These were the icons of youth culture in 1970s Korea. The creators and consumers of this culture were none other than college students. Armed with the shared sensibility and tastes of the new generation, they stood at the forefront of the trends and patterns in popular music, film, and books. University campuses at the time were often fogged with tear gas, but folk music was also an important part of activism, which gradually made its way into mainstream radio waves.

At the same time, students were the most outspoken critics of youth culture. Campus newspapers, including the *Ewha Weekly*, defined youth culture as a tainted and decadent foreign import, rejecting the notion that it represented university culture. Authentic campus culture was rooted in anti-establishment grassroots activism, they asserted, advocating the legacy of Korean mask dance, farmers' music and other traditional genres.

However, youth culture at the time had less to do with style and appearance, like dressing in jeans and growing your hair, than the spirit of resistance, as a critic pointed out. It was more than a one-time fad derived from imitations of Western culture, representing freedom and liberation in the face of outmoded values and conventions that imposed control and conformity.

Ewha's students had always been trendsetters in culture and fashion, and the streets outside the campus gates were lined with the city's most popular boutiques, salons and shops. The area came to be called the new Myeongdong, after the central shopping district downtown, always bustling with crowds. This brought about criticism that Ewha's trendy women endorsed extravagance, but the author Choi In-ho, a leading voice of the youth culture generation, spoke out in defense:

> The reason Ewha students look so pretty is, as President Kim Okgill pointed out, because they're young, not because they indulge in luxury. They're bright, fit, full of smiles, and have healthy appetites—business is thriving at a shop that

: Ewha's students on the campus during the 1970s.

sells 10-won plates of fried squid in the neighborhood—so I know they would have looked fabulous even if they were dressed in rags.

- *The Hankook Ilbo Daily*, May 22, 1974

Whatever people might say about their styles, Ewha's students strode across the campus in their bell-bottoms and mini-skirts, their long hair waving in the wind. The sight they created as they crossed the Ewha Bridge inside the main gate in throngs became an attraction for visitors. It was also an intimidating experience for men to walk through this crowd, and male visitors were often seen lingering outside the gate, which created rumors that men were not allowed on the Ewha campus.

In addition to the fashionable storefronts, the streets around Ewha boasted quaint, romantic spots like the Paris Tearoom and the Eine Kleine Music Room, where many generations of Ewha students had left behind memories of their youth.

1979

1990

VI
The Leap Forward

Ewha Renaissance

: Science Building

Center of Education and Research

In the fall of 1979, the new semester opened at Ewha with an air of anticipation surrounding the inauguration of its 9th president Chung Ii-Sook. President Kim Okgill had submitted her resignation to the Faculty Council and the Ewha Haktang Foundation several months earlier and Chung was unanimously supported as the right leader to steer the school toward change in the new decade. She had built up experience as an administrator in her roles as dean in both undergraduate and graduate programs and had also been at the helm of many successful university events.

At the time, a long military dictatorship had come to an end, but was followed by social and political turmoil, the university campuses also swept up in the chaos. In the spring of

1980, young men and women poured out into the streets of Seoul, staging a defiant struggle in defense of democracy. Despite resistance, another military regime seized power, and feeling threatened by student activism, the government attempted to limit the autonomy of universities and to keep the minds and hands of young intellects under control by executing oppressive measures to minimize the social influence of universities, mainly through the Graduation Quota System. Under this new policy, universities were required to admit more students than the designated graduation quota, then hold back or fail students with the lowest grades. Stiff competition came to dominate the mood at universities around the country, the spirit of exploration and truth-seeking taking second seat.

Such times called for a serious inquiry into the role and mission of the university, into the question of how the university should respond to the times. President Chung Ii-Sook proposed as the new slogan for Ewha, "University as Center of Education and Research." Ewha had endured the turmoil of the 1960s and 70s with support from its long tradition and history, and now it was time to make the next leap forward as not merely a women's university but one with the caliber of a top-class educational institution.

Becoming a center of education and research meant creating the optimal environment for student learning and for

: Inauguration ceremony for Ewha's 9th President Chung Ii-Sook (1979).

faculty research, which required the restoration of the true function of a university. First of all Ewha set out to increase the number of its faculty to secure outstanding professors, and to reorganize and strengthen its research institutes. Graduate programs sought out specific disciplines to develop at Ewha, which resulted in the establishment of the Department of Women's Studies and the Department of Korean Studies in 1982, contributing greatly to creating a new academic tradition.

During this time, construction continued non-stop on the campus, bringing big improvements to Ewha's educational infrastructure. The new buildings included the Music Building, the Admission Hall, the Science Building, the Law Building and the Ewha Centennial Library, while the Alumnae Building and the Education Building were expanded. The changes sought to maximize the use of space, resulting in more effective administration and an enhanced academic atmosphere.

President Chung's most prized construction project was the university library, for which she envisioned an optimal structure for the increased student population and sought advice from specialists on every detail, from spatial layout to the sizes of the chairs and tables, before commissioning the design. A five-year acquisition plan was established to fill the new library stacks, which was carried out meticulously, securing 1 million titles in time for the opening. In 1984, the Ewha Centennial

Ewha Centennial Library (1984).

Library opened, equipped with state-of-the-art facilities and operated by an effective management system, receiving wide recognition as one of the most outstanding university libraries in the country. To this day it stands proud atop the campus's hill, its facade white and magnificent against the backdrop of the lush woods.

Promise of Lifelong Education for Women

As more and more women are seeking opportunities to pursue further learning in their middle age, Ewha Womans University has opened its School of Continuing Education, to offer courses to housewives and working women starting in the spring of 1984. While continuing education until now has been provided by social organizations, Ewha's new program will offer university-level courses within a systematic and sustaining curriculum. It is also a novel approach that college education, once reserved for the young for a limited period of time, is now offered to a broad age group, and by a wider range of institutions.

- *The Donga Ilbo Daily*, November 28, 1983

As national newspapers reported, in 1983 Ewha Womans University opened the School of Continuing Education, becoming the first university in Korea to establish a venue to offer adult learning opportunities.

When applications opened for the inaugural classes for the spring of 1984, housewives arrived in throngs, seeking courses in liberal arts or professional training. One of the most popular courses were the 40-student English class and the 50-student course, "Psychology in Everyday Life," which were filled the first day of registration, and almost all the other classes had to turn away a number of applicants.

Ewha's School of Continuing Education aimed at enriching the intellectual and cultural lives of women; enhancing women's social contribution and providing better jobs for women; and producing more educated women who will contribute to solving problems in local communities. Its curriculum was offered in three categories to reflect this vision: Liberal Arts, Professional Training and Social Volunteer Work.

Admission was open to all regardless of education or age, and students were issued certificates upon completing a given program. The school's first certification ceremony took place in August 1985, one year and six months after its establishment, with certification presented to 36 students in the Administration in Children's Education program and one student in the

: Ewha opens School of Continuing Education (1983).

Liberal Arts program.

Continuing education was one of President Chung's top initiatives upon taking office, in the spirit of Ewha's founding vision of social contribution and compassion. The establishment of the School of Continuing Education was proposed in her inauguration speech as one of her seven major projects, emphasizing increased education opportunities for women and enhanced quality of life by providing affordable learning.

It was Ewha's calling to open wide the university's doors for the society at large, as an institution founded on compassion and commitment.

A Century of Dreams

Throughout the month of May in 1986, Ewha's centennial year, a special song was sung at every chapel service:

> We have gathered today in Ewha's glorious gardens
> Flowers of truth spread their scent all around
> Bringing love to our thorny red-soil path.
> Girls, you have acquired light through learning.
> Now behold.
> The hope of a hundred years
> The faith of a hundred years
> The glory of a hundred years
> Ah-ah we shall uphold in Ewha's name.

"The dream of a hundred years/the fulfillment of a hundred

: Ewha's centennial celebrations (1986).

years/the joy of a hundred years/ah-ah preserve them forever in Ewha's wisdom." The lyrics to the Ewha Centennial Ode engraved pride and exhilaration in the hearts of everyone in the community.

Ewha's first century marked a long journey that traced the many turns in the history of modern Korea and its women. As President Chung Ii-Sook stressed in her centennial commemoration speech, those 100 years were a record of "a history in pursuit of the humanization of women," and "a testimony to the great human potential." At the centennial ceremony, the Ewha community reflected on the spirit that had been passed down over the course of the century, and recollected the dedicated service that made this proud history possible. It was an occasion for acknowledging Ewha's traditions, for expressing gratitude to its neighbors, and for making new pledges for a hopeful future.

The centennial celebrations were not just for the Ewha community, for its history had not been made on its own. Guests from near and far participated in commemorating Ewha's achievements, for which many were awarded with honorary degrees and appreciation plaques. Other festivities included academic conferences and special commemorative projects like the issuing of the Modern Women's Education Centennial Stamp in collaboration with the Ministry of Communications, which was especially notable as an official recognition from the government of Ewha's contribution to women's education and Korea's modernization.

The centennial was a new beginning for Ewha as it prepared for the 21st century following the university's tremendous growth and the great strides achieved in Korea politically, economically and socially in the late 1980s. The new era called for new directions in education, and the university launched the Ewha Development Task Force Committee to put together a comprehensive master plan, with an aim to soar higher in Ewha's next century.

Cultural Tug-of-War

In celebration of Ewha's centennial, the students organized the Grand National Harmony Festival under the slogan, "Ewha, Embrace Your History and Awaken to the Call of the Nation." Festivities featured a wide range of performances, exhibitions and athletic activities hosted by respective colleges and clubs, and also modern interpretations of traditional farmers' music and shaman rituals, tug-of-war and torchlight ceremonies, to pray for harmony that would bring democratization to Korea.

The centennial festival took on special significance since it was organized by the university-wide Student Council, launched a year before after a long period of being controlled by the Students' Corps for National Protection, a state-regulated organization.

The Students' Corps for National Protection was first established in 1949 to effectively manage student unrest amidst political turmoil following Korea's liberation from Japan, which in 1960 was transformed into the Student Union as a result of the April 19 Revolution. Under the Yusin military dictatorship in the 1970s, however, student bodies around the country were once again reorganized under the system of the Students' Corps for National Protection. It was in 1983, when campus deregulation measures were initiated, that students formed alliances to abolish the oppressive and controlling Students' Corps and to revive autonomous student representation. At Ewha, the new Student Council was officially launched in 1985 through an election participated by 73.4% of the student population, supported by over 50% of the votes, reflecting the students' high anticipation for the new student body. Autonomy in student activity was soon regained through a reorganization process that established specialized executive bodies and subcommittees, allowing close attention to student needs and voices.

The biggest difference brought about by the new Student Council was encouraged student activity and as a result the students took charge of the school festivities. As seen in the new title, the Grand National Harmony Festival, the Student Council planned the spring festival as a creative and autonomous event emphasizing unity in spirit, gearing away from the

Ewha's student-organized Grand National Harmony Festival.

Yeongsan Tug-of-War, highlight of the spring festival.

elitist and consumerist tastes that once defined Ewha culture to revive the traditional communal festivities featuring performances and rituals and games like farmers' music, mask dance and tug-of-war.

The Yeongsan Tug-of-War was the highlight of the spring festival. Originating from the Yeongsan region in Southern Gyeongsang Province, this folk game was held on the festival's last day on the athletic field, participated by thousands of students to create a scene filled with drama and energy. Preparations for the game kicked off with a well-wishing ritual several days before the festival, with students joining hands to make rope by twisting and braiding straw, to be used on the day of the game. And on the festival's last day, hundreds of students took part in the tug-of-war, the excitement escalating amidst the cheering and singing. In the end, the game gradually shifted to dancing and singing and a torch march to wrap up the events. Today Ewha is the only university to carry on the tradition of the Yeongsan Tug-of-War, which still makes up the core of the festival program, along with the Ganggangsullae Circle Dance, another traditional activity, introduced in 2005.

Ewha's Grand National Harmony Festival has been a showcase of traditional culture mixed with modern elements, reflecting the change of times each year. As a result, Ewha has been able to offer exciting crowd-pleasing programs without the help of corporate sponsorship or popular celebrities, successfully instilling a sense of identity, belonging and camaraderie as members of the Ewha community, with eyes in the same direction, harboring the same dreams.

Witnessed at the Ewha Centennial Grand National Harmony Festival was not only the roar of the Ewha students in action but also their dreams for the new century ahead.

1990s

Present

VII

Ewha in the 21st Century

Global Dreams and Challenges

Ewha Campus Complex

Model for the 21st Century

The Korean society in the 1990s was experiencing a period of sweeping change in politics, economy, culture and lifestyle. With the 21st century around the corner, it was a time when borders were being taken down between nations, paving the way for the transfer and integration of all resources.

In September of 1990, the Ewha campus was also swept up in the wave of change as Yoon Hoo Jung took office as the university's 10th president, the first to be appointed through direct election. The life that Yoon had led, as a legal scholar of integrity and as an outspoken intellectual, set high expectations for her role at Ewha's helm, to lead its future towards democratic reforms.

The new president put forth two immediate tasks for Ewha

in times of globalization: to achieve quality growth as a research university; and to seek Ewha's unique path in the worldwide pursuit of globalization. Upon taking office, President Yoon launched the Ewha 21st-Century Development Planning Committee and the University Development Committee, with a view to establishing Ewha's blueprint for the coming century, proposing 100 tasks that need to be addressed for Ewha to make the leap towards a world-class university.

Her vision and master plan were made public on Ewha's 108th anniversary day on national television, in a program on the Korea Broadcasting System titled "Grand Feast for Ewha's Leap into 21st Century." On the show, President Yoon emphasized the importance of cultivating professional women capable of competing internationally, defining the new Ewha model as the "integrated woman."

The integrated woman actively and independently participates in politics and history and carries out one's role in this world as a human being, transcending gender distinction in thought, values, ability and function. More specifically, Yoon broke down the concept into four categories: the woman as possessor of talent and virtue; the woman as a whole being; the woman for the global era, armed with creativity and professionalism; and the woman as mother of nation and history, a healer of social conflicts.

: Inauguration ceremony for Ewha's 10th President Yoon Hoo Jung (1990).

: Grand Feast for Ewha's Leap into 21st Century (1994).

The concept was reintroduced this time to emphasize the need for a new model for the Ewha woman, gifted with both talent and virtue, while upholding the university's traditional spirit of truth, goodness and beauty. The theory of the integrated woman for the new times, in other words, was one based on pluralistic integration that accepts and embraces difference, and also a new humanization strategy for the global era. The concept of the "integrated woman," as proposed by President Yoon, served as the guidepost for Ewha's development.

Toward the Humanization of Women Around the World

Ewha has throughout its history embraced its role as a pioneer for the humanization of Korean women and as the birthplace of women's studies in Korea. Its founding vision to humanize women reflects empathy for the painful lives that women of this country endured under oppression and inequality, and the determination to overcome the legacy.

Since offering Korea's first university course on women's studies in 1977, Ewha has gone on to establish graduate programs in the discipline, offering all levels of degrees, thereby achieving theoretic generalization and structure while contributing to the field's advancement through interdisciplinary research.

The first women's studie's course, offered as part of the un-

: Ewha offered Korea's first women's studies course.

dergraduate liberal arts curriculum, was taught in a fresh new format that incorporated team teaching, debates, plays and interviews, to explore a range of topics including "women and literature" and "women and history." Word quickly spread among students, and the scene of students lined up at 5 a.m. to sign up for the course was even featured in the national media. The course helped Ewha's students contemplate their own identities and cast their eyes beyond gender inequality to the contradictions within social systems. Their introduction to women's studies reaffirmed the students of their social responsibility toward the lives of women at large, not only their own, and of Ewha's raison d'etre as a women's university.

In 1977, the Center for Women's Studies was established at Ewha, which was reorganized and expanded in 1995 as the Korean Women's Institute (KWI), and led to the founding of the Asian Center for Women's Studies. The center's publications, including *The History of Korean Women* and *Sourcebook on Relations of Korean Women* help introduce the discipline to Korea, while KWI's project to publish *Sourcebook on Women's History in Korea: The Annals of the Joseon Dynasty* contributed greatly to the advancement of research in the field. Researchers and scholars from home and abroad frequented the institute's squeaky wooden quarters on the Ewha campus to plan and discuss new projects, confirming KWI's status as the birthplace of women's studies in Korea and a hub for international research in the field.

Ewha has served as a leader in the field of women's studies and activism through its efforts in developing new discourses in women's issues, opening new horizons in women's education by producing world-class researchers in the field. Ewha is also contributing to the globalization of women's studies by helping building an alliance of women's studies scholars and activists around Asia, creating an academic community that reaches far beyond Korea. In this new age of women in the 21st century, led by women taking charge in the efforts to open a new era of gender equality, women's studies at Ewha stands at the frontier of women's development, welfare and rights, as it continues its journey as pioneer and creator.

In June 2005, during President Shin In-ryung's term in office, the Ewha campus fulfilled its role as the mecca of women's studies when it hosted the 9th Women's Worlds congress. Participated by some 3,000 scholars from over 100 countries, the international conference was held for six days in various venues around Sinchon including Yonsei and Sogang Universities. It was the first time an Asian university hosted the conference and the largest to date. As stated by Ewha professor Chang Pil-wha, who served as the director of the organization committee, the occasion was "an opportunity to show the world the improved

: 9th Women's Worlds congress (2005).

status of women in Korea and the socio-cultural capacities of the Korean society."

In 2006, Ewha launched a program that would allow it to give back to the world the fruits it had reaped. Titled the Ewha Global Partnership Program (EGPP), the program selects a total of 120 women from developing countries to attend undergraduate or graduate programs at Ewha, providing full tuition, living expense and support for Korean-language courses. In its inaugural year, 24 students—three doctoral, eight master's and 13 undergraduate students—were selected from 15 countries, including Vietnam, Afghanistan, Cambodia, Mozambique and Kenya, drawing much attention from the press. They traveled to Korea, an unfamiliar country on the other side of the world, in pursuit of their dreams. Utui Nadia, from Mozambique, said she planned to "study architecture in order to build strong houses and bridges in my homeland where many buildings have been destroyed by war," while Rasouli Zahra, from Afghanistan, declared ambitiously that she dreams of "becoming Afghanistan's first woman president after majoring in women's studies and human rights."

The program upholds the spirit of Ewha founder Mary F. Scranton, who began women's education 120 years ago in the distant, unknown land of Joseon, and aims at giving back to the world's women the capacities that Ewha has accumulated

Welcoming festival for Ewha Global Partnership Program students during Ewha 120th anniversary celebrations (2006).

Participants from around the world in the Ewha Global Partnership Program.

over the years. As is evident in the title, the program is a partnership project, not a one-way dispensation of goodwill, which speaks for the university's goal of working in harmony and cooperation with the women of the world. EGPP is also proof that Ewha's vision to become a global hub for women's education in pursuit of the humanization of women has now found its path in the world.

With its vision for the 21st century focusing on cultivating dynamic women leaders for the new era, Ewha has taken decisive steps in reforming outdated traditions. An example is the abolition of the ban on student marriage. Back in 1946, Ewha included a clause in the statutes of the university that admission to the school is "limited to unmarried women," which aimed at prohibiting students from getting married while enrolled as a student. The clause was added during the college's early years to prevent students from giving up their studies for marriage, a move that was necessary for securing women's right to pursue an education under dire circumstances. As time passed, however, Ewha's marriage ban had been a source of heated debate and in 2003, was finally abolished.

Following the decision, over 20 women who had been expelled upon marriage returned to school, their ages ranging from the 30s to the 70s. Anecdotes about their return to campus drew public attention and media coverage—of getting

Elderly students return to school following the abolition of the ban on student marriage (2003).

lost amidst the unfamiliar new buildings; of the difficulty they faced in communicating with the young students in class discussions; of struggling with computer technology only to end up losing entire term papers on the hard drive.

Research at Ewha: Specialization and Focus

"Graduate student publishes paper in *Science*!" (*Kyunghyang Shinmun*, February 16, 2003)
"Ph.D. candidate publishes 'Electro-tunable optical diode based on photonic bandgap liquid-crystal heterojunctions' in *Nature Materials* as 1st author" (*The Hankyoreh*, April 24, 2005)
"Master's student publishes 'Regulation of PDGF signaling and vascular remodeling by peroxiredoxin II' in *Nature* as 1st author" (*The Hankyoreh*, May 19, 2005)

In the early 2000s, Korea's national media published a series of reports about notable scientific research accomplished by graduate students, focusing on the fact that the students were all from Ewha. Their achievements were results of the investments made by Ewha as part of its initiative to advance into a world-class university, only the first sprouts budding from seeds that had been sown ten years earlier.

It was no coincidence that in 1996, Ewha established the world's first engineering college for women. Despite opinions that time was not ripe yet, considering the school's financial situation and social atmosphere, President Yoon Hoo Jung persistently pushed the plan, bluntly asserting her views: "It is not as if women have been programmed to be incapable of executing certain types of work." She had foreseen that women could fall behind in the global competition of the future unless they equip themselves with specialized knowledge, and that in order for Ewha to rise above the limits of a women's school and establish itself as a balanced and comprehensive university, a focus on the sciences was crucial.

Ewha continued to develop strategies to enhance its capacities in life science, information technology and international trade. Bold investments were made in the field of life science after concluding that women had a competitive edge considering that many possessed the attributes that the field requires—creativity, precision and affinity to living beings.

Ewha's initiative to grow as a specialized research university for women was accelerated by the establishment of professional and specialized graduate schools. President Chang Sang's term

Ewha establishes world's first engineering college for women (1996).

in office saw a rapid increase in the number of new graduate schools, including the Graduate School of International Studies and the Graduate School of Translation and Interpretation, which aim at producing professional women for the global era; the Graduate School of Theology, the first of its kind for women in Korea; and the Graduate School of Policy Science. Other schools later followed, strengthening Ewha's research foundation and capacities, including the School of Medicine, the Ewha School of Business, and Ewha Law School.

This was the backdrop against which the Division of Molecular and Life Sciences was established in 1998, followed by the founding of the Institute of Life Science and Technology, and the recruitment of Dr. Rhee Sue Goo, a world-renowned scientist in the field at Seoul National University, by President Chang, who persuaded him with an innovative proposal and the promise of unprecedented support. The division grew remarkably under the helm of Distinguished Professor Rhee, leading to the establishment of the Division of Nano Science in 2003 upon the hiring, both as Distinguished Professors, of Dr. Sohn Youn Soo of the Korea Institute of Science and Technology and world-acclaimed chemist Dr. Choy Jin-Ho of Seoul National University.

What is interesting is that when Ewha began producing results internationally, the media set out to analyze what had

Center for Cell Signaling Research established (1998).

Scranton College established (2007).

enabled this leap. One of the reports pointed out the unique operation system at the two divisions, based on "openness and concentration." The Division of Molecular Life Science and Technology houses all of its researchers and facilities under one roof, a five-story building with a two-story basement constructed in 2004. The entire floor space on each floor is completely open, without walls to divide the different labs, and its main facilities located in the center, to be shared by some 20 faculty members. The layout calls for constant interaction and discussion among the researchers. These efforts are what resulted in the remarkable number of papers and the contribution of graduate students in major research published in prestigious journals.

In 2008, the new five-story engineering building, with three underground floors and covering an area of 10,578m^2, was competed, greatly enhancing the research infrastructure at the College of Engineering. During the tenure of President Lee Bae Yong, Scranton College was launched, offering Korea's first individually-designed major to provide an interdisciplinary and convergent education, with all courses taught in English.

Global Time, Global Space

On her way to class, A, a sophomore at Ewha Womans University, checks the school app on her smart phone for new notices regarding the course. As she steps inside the classroom, she uses her bar-coded multifunction ID card to check attendance. During class, she downloads lecture notes on her tablet PC and saves her own notes on the file. Then she logs on to the library database to search for papers and other information for her assignment. Signing on to the EUREKA on-line system, she takes care of administrative tasks without having to leave the room.

The conveniences that students enjoy on the Ewha campus today were unthinkable a few years ago. The state-of-the-art network system, which Ewha began building in the 1990s, has brought about a shift in Ewha's time and spatial structures to those of the future. Ewha embarked on the project to create a high-tech virtual campus before any other university in Korea, connecting the entire school community and infrastructure by a single comprehensive information network, which evolved from the ETIS, the Ewhanet, and the Ewhanet gigabit high-speed network, into the Ewha Portal Information System, or EPIS, and most recently, the EUREKA system.

In the 1990s, new buildings began going up all over the campus, completely transforming the school grounds. Among them, the Ewha Campus Complex (ECC), which began construction in 2005 and was completed in 2008, was the most ambitious project, symbolizing the new possibilities that await Ewha's future. Designed by renowned French architect Dominique Perrault, ECC is a high-tech six-floor basement facility, the biggest of its kind in Korea, covering an area of 66,000m^2. The building's middle section cuts through like a valley, forming a long stretch of open space that leads to a wide and steep stairway comprising 130 steps, which function as a public plaza.

What is most notable about the facility is that it serves as a venue for a learning community, the latest trend in campus design. Students come here for class, carry on a discussion with classmates in the lounge, then move on to lunch, to the gym,

Ewha Campus Complex and its reading rooms (2008).

or choose to catch a movie or a play, all in the same building, a one-stop campus that connects learning, life and culture. ECC has enhanced the campus experience for Ewha's students, functioning as a future-oriented educational facility that adds a global competitive edge.

With these new developments, the students of Ewha can experience the historical structures side by side with the 21st-century additions, witnessing the encounter between the past and the present and the summoning of history to the scene of our current lives.

Ewha has also been establishing a global campus comprised of an open network of partner schools around the world. This network is supplemented by Ewha's exchange student program, which has for a long time contributed to the internationalization of the students. The number of outgoing exchange students from Ewha dramatically increased in the 1990s, returning with the skills and experiences required for international professions. Today over 1,500 students a year head out to different parts of the world including the U.S., the U.K., Canada, Australia, Japan, Germany and China, promoting Ewha's name in different corners of the world.

Visits by notable figures from around the world are also the result of Ewha's efforts in international exchange and creating openness. They include Britain's Queen Elizabeth II; world-

U.S. Secretary of State Hillary Clinton visits Ewha (2009).

renowned primatologist Jane Goodall; U.S. Ambassador to Korea Kathleen Stephens; President Michelle Bachelet of Chile; U.S. Secretary of State Hillary Clinton; Germany's Chancellor Angela Merkel; Thailand's Prime Minister Yingluck Shinawatra; Silvia Renate Sommerlath, Queen of Sweden; Drew Gilpin Faust, President of Harvard University; and Tarja Kaarina Halonen, Former President of Finland. These distinguished guests admired the beautiful campus and the outstanding educational environment at Ewha, expressing deep interest in the students who are in preparation for a future as Korea's leaders.

Ewha has presented the Distinguished Honorary Ewha Fellowship to Hillary Clinton and Harvard University's first woman president Drew Gilpin Faust, in acknowledgement of their achievements as international woman leaders, an inspiration to Ewha's vision of challenge and ambition. The Distinguished Honorary Ewha Fellowship is an honor presented to accomplished dignitaries from outside the Ewha community who have contributed significantly to the enhancement of women's rights. Such occasions have immensely enhanced Ewha's global image and strengthened its reputation as a global institution dedicated to making contributions to the world.

: Chancellor of Germany Angela Merkel awarded honorary doctoral degree from Ewha (2010).

Ewha, Where Change Begins: The Global Hub for Women's Education

Current president Kim Sun-Uk took office in 2010, embracing the weight and responsibility of Ewha's proud legacy with a vision to create "an open academic community that provides guideposts to society." The spirit that the university is pursuing in these times is represented by the slogan, "Ewha, Where Change Begins." The change will be one brought about by the course of action taken in the three following directions: Ambitious Ewha; Global Ewha; Communal Ewha.

Ambitious Ewha represents President Kim's vision for a world-class research university. The school has pledged extensive support for outstanding research and for promising new projects, an example of which is the recent agreement signed with the global chemical corporation Solvay to build the Ewha-

: Ewha and Solvay sign agreement for cooperation in research and development (2011).

Solvay Global R&D Center, the first instance of a multinational firm jointly establishing an R&D facility with a Korean university. The agreement speaks for Ewha's outstanding research capacity, including faculty and patents, and will serve as an opportunity to take it to the next level.

The Ewha Global Top 5 Project also aims at enhancing research at Ewha by investing 10 billion won in research funds over the course of three years in the most promising areas. Ewha has served as a pioneer in Korea's history of women in science, producing the country's first woman physician and the first woman scientist, and now a new generation of students is aspiring to become the next Marie Curie.

Global Ewha is a reminder of the university's responsibility as the global hub for women's education. Throughout its history, Ewha has produced women pioneers in myriad fields who have overcome the bounds and limitations imposed on Korean women. Now Ewha is responding to the demands of the changing times by looking beyond Korea to carry out its role as the global hub for women's education, a new vision rooted in the sense of responsibility to spread Ewha's spirit of challenge, of service and sharing, embedded in its time-honored history.

To this end, Ewha has opened its Global Service Center for international students and faculty, and launched the Ewha Global Partnership Program, the Ewha-KOICA Master's Program in International Studies, and the Ewha Global Empowerment Program, each aimed at strengthening global networks through the support of women activists and workers from Asia and Africa. The Ewha-KF Global e-School program, which provides on-line courses and seminars on Korean studies to students at universities around the world, is also an attempt at connecting the women of the world through education. In President Kim's own words, Ewha will now serve as stepping stones for talented women at home and abroad, just as the missionaries had done some 120 years ago.

The change in Ewha's role, from the cradle of education for Korean women to the global hub for women's education, is based on Ewha's social responsibility, to bring true change for all. Women leaders from around the world are now forming strong regional and global alliances, with Ewha at the center of their efforts to realize women's values, and together they will contribute greatly to changing the direction of social and human development by overcoming poverty and improving women's rights.

Communal Ewha is about reviving the spirit of service and sharing by establishing a healthy local community joined by love and dedication. In 1998, Ewha initiated the Social Volunteer Credit System, which offered social volunteer courses connected with each major, promoting volunteer work and

: Participants in the Ewha Global Empowerment Program for women leaders from developing countries.

social participation by students. The system was expanded in 2008 into the Social Volunteer Certification System to better keep track of various volunteer activities by Ewha students. Combining volunteer work with coursework has proven highly effective in cultivating professionals as whole beings and in pushing the students to prove their self-worth as world citizens. One evident result is the increased number of student clubs at Ewha focused on volunteer work for the disabled, like Civitan, the Howoo Society and the Sonji Club.

Other community-related projects include the Ewha Unity and Communication Campaign, aimed at promoting communication within the Ewha community; the Scent of Love from Ewha project, which offers support for senior citizens living alone in the Seodaemun and Mapo districts; the Ewha Community's *Pro Bono* Activities project and the Ewha Eco Shop, which sells recycled goods donated by members of the Ewha community. The university has also opened the Ewha Social Service in Cambodia to support children and teenage girls from low-income families, the first of its kind established by a Korean university.

Non Nobis Solum. As quoted by President Kim Sun-Uk in her inauguration speech, these words by Roman philosopher Cicero emphasize that we at Ewha do not exist for ourselves alone but for the community at large. Ewha's new spirit is about carrying out its responsibilities as a university that serves the society. Ewha's time-honored mission to serve and share, and its spirit of compassion and justice, preserved for over a century with courage and determination, is now spreading from within the community to our neighbors and throughout the world. This is where change begins, for Ewha, for our neighbors, and the world at large.

Epilogue

> Ewha Womans University aims at achieving the humanization of women, a goal rooted in Christian values and the education philosophy of the Republic of Korea, thereby contributing to the advancement of the nation and mankind through the education of women to build character and knowledge, through forward-looking pursuits in academic research and dedicated social service.
>
> - Article 1, Charter of Ewha Womans University

The first article of the Charter of Ewha Womans University reflects Ewha's educational goal and philosophy, underlining its identity as an institution for higher education and its role as a women's university. It contains the history that Ewha has created for women's education in Korea, while illuminating its present and its vision for the future.

The history of Ewha, which began in May 1886 with a single student, was one of dedication and commitment to the cause of the humanization of women; one of challenges and of overcoming those challenges. The women of Ewha chose to write history rather than create myths, each of their stories making up a single splendid legacy. The miracle of Ewha is the result of this legacy and of the determination and responsibility to uphold every mission and calling with pride and dignity. The spirit of Ewha, realized through the mission of the humanization of women and the Christian philosophy of truth, goodness and beauty, has been passed down for over a century, serving as the guidepost for the university through the changing times.

It was the Christian faith that first brought light on the women of this country in the 19th century during a dark age for women's education, and Ewha has since played the role of an adventurous and successful pioneer. At Ewha, the young girls of Korea who were not even given their own names, received an education to become pioneers in the early days of modernization, carrying out their mission to share and to serve as leaders in their fields. Ewha also sought independence in the face of brutal oppression from the Japanese colonialists, and during the war, amidst earth-shaking gunfire, turned its passion for learning into miracles.

In times of political turmoil on Korea's path toward democracy, Ewha at times stood at the forefront in the fight against the system, but also reaffirmed its responsibilities as the center of learning and in the pursuit of truth and wisdom. While upholding the role of women as socially-conscious intellectuals and as agents of revolutionary change, Ewha's women at the same time sought academic answers to the question of how women can co-exist in the world with men.

Now in this era of globalization, Ewha stands on the threshold of moving beyond the effort for the humanization of Korean women and making the leap into a world-class university. As forward-looking world citizens, the entire Ewha community is working to bring about change for all. Today, the spirit of Ewha lies in love and sharing, in co-existence and cooperation, in giving back to the women of the world the educational capacities that Ewha has accumulated in the course of the humanization of women.

Ewha is home to myriad women of global capacities who are challenging the future in their pursuit of the dream to change the world: creative young women equipped with multicultural and multilingual capacities; women dedicated to building social capital; intellectuals of outstanding character practicing the Christian spirit. As an open academic community, Ewha has also taken on the role of stepping stones for women around the world.

Today Ewha continues to move forward, looking toward the state of women around the world, taking its past into the future, across the border between Korea and the world. Ewha will lead the spirit of the times forward, just as it has done in the past, setting its own standards to serve as the proof of hope, thereby creating a history of change and possibility.

Chronology

1886	Ewha Haktang opens as Korea's first educational institution for women.
1887	Boguyeogwan opens as Korea's first hospital exclusively serving women.
1910	College courses offered at Ewha Haktang.
1914	Ewha Haktang produces Korea's first women to earn undergraduate degrees.
1925	Ewha College founded.
1935	Ewha campus moves to Sinchon.
1943	Ewha Haktang Educational Foundation established.
1946	Ewha Womans University becomes Korea's first university to receive official government accreditation.
1950	Ewha Womans University Graduate School established.
1951	Ewha opens evacuee campus in Busan following the outbreak of the Korean War.
1963	Ewha Womans University Graduate School awards its first doctoral degrees.

1977	Korea's first women's studies course offered at Ewha.
1986	Ewha's 100th anniversary.
1995	Ewha ranks top place in Comprehensive University Accreditation System conducted by the Korean Council for University Education.
1996	Ewha establishes world's first women's engineering college.
2004	Ewha ranks top place in 2nd Comprehensive University Accreditation System conducted by the Korean Council for University Education.
2006	Ewha Global Partnership Program launched.
2007	Scranton College established.
2008	Ewha Campus Complex opens as Korea's largest environment–friendly underground campus.
2011	Ewha signs university-industry collaboration agreement with global chemical group Solvay.
2012	Ewha Global Empowerment Program launched for women serving in non-government public sectors around Asia and Africa. Ewha named host of Institute for Basic Science (IBS) West Seoul Center.
2013	Ranked 1st among Korean universities in CWTS Leiden Ranking, measuring the scientific performances of 500 major universities worldwide. Ewha launches its Residential College program. Construction begins for the Ewha University–Industry Collaboration Center.

The Story of Ewha

From History to Future

Written by Ewha Archives
Translated by Jung Ha-yun

Jung Ha-yun is a member of the faculty at Ewha Womans University's Graduate School of Translation and Interpretation. Her writing and translations have been supported by the Radcliffe Institute for Advanced Study at Harvard University; the Literature Translation Institute of Korea; and the PEN American Center.

First published October 17, 2013
by Ewha Womans University Press
52, Ewhayeodae-gil, Seodaemun-gu, Seoul, Korea 120-750
Tel.: 82-2-3277-2965, 362-6076 / Fax.: 82-2-312-4312
E-mail: press@ewha.ac.kr
Homepage: www.ewhapress.com

Price: 16,000 won
ISBN 978-89-7300-989-3 03900